Less Web Development Essentials

Second Edition

Second Edition

Leverage the features of Less to write better, reusable, and maintainable CSS code

Bass Jobsen

PUBLISHING

BIRMINGHAM - MUMBAI

Less Web Development Essentials
Second Edition

First published: April 2014

Second edition: April 2015

Production reference: 1270415

Published by Packt Publishing Ltd.
Livery Place
35 Livery Street
Birmingham B3 2PB, UK.

ISBN 978-1-78355-407-2

www.packtpub.com

Credits

Author

Bass Jobsen

Reviewers

Ben Burwell

Shahin Katebi

Maulik Suchak

Xun (Brian) Wu

Acquisition Editor

Tushar Gupta

Content Development Editor

Sriram Neelakantan

Technical Editors

Novina Kewalramani

Shruti Rawool

Copy Editors

Jasmine Nadar

Alpha Singh

Trishla Singh

Laxmi Subramanian

Neha Vyas

Project Coordinator

Judie Jose

Proofreaders

Safis Editing

Paul Hindle

Indexer

Tejal Soni

Production Coordinator

Alwin Roy

Cover Work

Alwin Roy

About the Author

Bass Jobsen has been programming for the Web since 1995, covering everything from C to PHP, and is always on the hunt for the most accessible interfaces. Based in Orthen, the Netherlands, he was the coauthor of *Less Web Development Cookbook, Packt Publishing*, which contains over 110 practical recipes to help you write leaner, more efficient CSS code using Less.

He uses Less in his daily job for web design tasks, WordPress theme development, the awesome StreetArt.nl project, and other Twitter Bootstrap apps.

He is always happy to help you at `http://stackoverflow.com/users/1596547/bass-jobsen`, and he blogs at `http://bassjobsen.weblogs.fm/`.

Also, check out his Bootstrap WordPress Starter Theme (JBST) and other projects on GitHub at `https://github.com/bassjobsen`.

Writing this book wouldn't have been possible without the support of my family. The entire team at Packt was helpful, specifically Tushar Gupta who was a patient and excellent motivator and critical reader. Sriram Neelakantan helped me to dot the *is* and cross the *ts*. I would also like to thank the reviewers of this book, Ben, Shahin, Maulik, and Xen (Brian), for their critical and valuable suggestions, which make this book even better.

Last but not least, I should not forget to thank the Less core team — Alexis Sellier (`@cloudhead`), Jon Schlinkert (`@jonschlinkert`), Luke Page (`@lukeapage`), Marcus Bointon (`@Synchro`), Mária Jurčovičová (`@sommeri`), Matthew Dean (`@matthew-dean`), Max Mikhailov (`@seven-phases-max`), and all the other contributors who have made coding Less possible in the first place.

About the Reviewers

Ben Burwell is a software engineer and web developer from Hopewell, New Jersey. He enjoys expression-oriented languages, security engineering, user interface design, and coffee. Ben also likes to spend time hiking, cooking, and enjoying fine typography. This is the first time he has reviewed a book for Packt Publishing. He has previously written about web and software development on his website (`https://www.benburwell.com/`).

Shahin Katebi is a software architect and developer with over 10 years of experience in creating apps for various platforms (Mac, iOS, Windows, and the Web). He works as a mobile solutions consultant with different companies in the business, marketing, and technical fields, and also works with start-up teams worldwide. He teaches iOS / Mac OS development and is a mentor at Startup Weekend events, where he helps start-up teams develop their own businesses. He is the founder and business manager of Seeb Co. (`http://seeb.co/`), a creative mobile app development organization that creates apps for customers around the world. He is also running and accelerating multiple start-up businesses in various fields worldwide.

Shahin has also helped with the fact checking and technical reviewing *iOS and OS X Network Programming Cookbook* and *PHPStorm Cookbook,* both by Packt Publishing.

I want to give my special thanks and love to my adorable Nafiseh for her treasured presence and support.

Maulik Suchak is a professional frontend developer and designer with over 6 years of experience. He is the cofounder of CVsIntellect.com, a résumé builder service.

He has also started an open source project called DearWeb.org (`https://github.com/ermauliks/dearweb.org`), a theme library that will help any non-frontend developer to write HTML/CSS. More information about him is available at `www.mauliksuchak.com`.

Xun (Brian) Wu is a software developer and a software architect with over 10 years of experience in a variety of industries, including financial services, information technology, entertainment, and sports.

His background is in Java, UI, and big data development.

He is always enthusiastic about exploring new ideas, technologies, and opportunities that arise. He always keeps himself up to date by reading books, attending trainings, and researching.

He has previously reviewed *Learning Express Web Application Development, Rapid LESS, Rapid Lo-Dash, Mastering D3.js, Mastering CSS, Mastering MEAN Web Development, Rapid Meteor, Mastering Kendo UI, Rapid Grunt*, and *Learning Flask*, all for Packt Publishing.

I would like to thank my parents, my wife, and my child for their patience and support throughout this endeavor.

www.PacktPub.com

Support files, eBooks, discount offers, and more

For support files and downloads related to your book, please visit www.PacktPub.com.

Did you know that Packt offers eBook versions of every book published, with PDF and ePub files available? You can upgrade to the eBook version at www.PacktPub.com and as a print book customer, you are entitled to a discount on the eBook copy. Get in touch with us at service@packtpub.com for more details.

At www.PacktPub.com, you can also read a collection of free technical articles, sign up for a range of free newsletters and receive exclusive discounts and offers on Packt books and eBooks.

https://www2.packtpub.com/books/subscription/packtlib

Do you need instant solutions to your IT questions? PacktLib is Packt's online digital book library. Here, you can search, access, and read Packt's entire library of books.

Why subscribe?

- Fully searchable across every book published by Packt
- Copy and paste, print, and bookmark content
- On demand and accessible via a web browser

Free access for Packt account holders

If you have an account with Packt at www.PacktPub.com, you can use this to access PacktLib today and view 9 entirely free books. Simply use your login credentials for immediate access.

This book is dedicated to Colinda, Kiki, Dries, Wolf, and Leny.

Table of Contents

Preface

Less (Leaner CSS) is a preprocessor, which means Less code compiles into static CSS code. Less changes the way you write and maintain your CSS code; the final CSS code will be the same, but better organized in many situations.

In your hands is the *Less Web Development Essentials, Second Edition* book. Since the successful first edition of this book, Less has been improved still further. This book has been updated for the all new features that come with the release of Less Version 2. The Less Version 2 release not only has many improvements, but has also introduced the possibility to use and write Less plugins. Less plugins will enable you to customize Less for your own unique needs.

In the semantic sense, valid CSS code is also valid Less code. Less tries to stay as close as possible to the declarative nature of CSS. Coding Less is intuitive and easy to learn for those who are already familiar with CSS.

Since the introduction of CSS3 in 2012, the role of CSS in modern web development has become more and more important. Nowadays, CSS3 is not only used to style your HTML documents, but also plays an important role in the responsibility of your designs. Last but not least, CSS3 extends CSS with features such as animations and transitions.

Writing correct functional CSS code will be the first thing—and keeping this code readable—working on all major browsers will be the second. CSS files grow and become untidy during the development and maintenance processes. CSS also doesn't have the ability to modify existing values or reuse common styles. Also, doing math or defining variables is not possible in CSS. This is where Less comes into the frame.

Less is a dynamic style sheet language designed by Alexis Sellier. Started in 2010 and now maintained and extended by the Less core team, it helps you make your CSS code maintainable, reusable, and also prevents code duplications. It also enables you to write your CSS code DRY (Do not Repeat Yourself), extending CSS syntax with variables, mixins, functions, and many other techniques. Less ensures that the CSS language is more maintainable, themable, and extendable.

In this book, you will learn to write, compile, and understand Less. We will help you to perform faster and more cost effective web development. You will get practical tips to integrate Less into your current and new projects. After reading this book, you will write clear and readable CSS3 with Less. Instead of spending your time debugging your complex CSS code for a specific device or browser, you can pay more attention to your real-design tasks.

Your clients will be happy with your advanced and stable designs. Development and maintenance time, along with expenditure, will decrease.

Also, other projects know the power of Less. Projects such as Twitter Bootstrap and the WordPress Roots theme rely on Less. These projects build clear and extendable frameworks with Less.

Less is open source and licensed under Apache License. The source code of Less is maintained on GitHub. Everybody will be allowed to contribute to it. You can use Less free of charge.

What this book covers

Chapter 1, Improving Web Development with Less, talks about how CSS3 brought web designers advanced functions such as gradients, transitions, and animations; however, it also stresses how CSS code can become more complex and difficult to maintain. Less helps you to make your CSS maintainable, reusable, and also prevents code duplications.

Chapter 2, Using Variables and Mixins, explains why variables allow you to specify widely used values in a single place and then reuse them throughout the style sheet, making global changes as easy as changing one line of code. Mixins allow you to embed all the properties of a class into another class by simply including the class name as one of its properties. It also explains what parametric mixins are and how to use them.

Chapter 3, Nested Rules, Operations, and Built-in Functions, explains how to use nested rules for making inheritance clear and creating shorter style sheets. It also shows you how to create complex relationships between properties and use the built-in functions of Less.

Chapter 4, Testing Your Code and Using Prebuilt Mixins Libraries, explains how to use well-written and tested Less code of third parties for your projects. Pre-built mixins and other sources help you to (re)use them.

Chapter 5, Integrating Less in Your Own Projects, explains how to organize your files for new projects or get the projects you maintain ready for using Less.

Chapter 6, Using the Bootstrap 3 Frontend Framework, explains how to use, customize, and extend Bootstrap with Less. Bootstrap is a popular CSS, HTML, and JavaScript framework to build mobile-first responsive designs.

Chapter 7, Less with External Applications and Frameworks, explains how to use other frameworks and grid systems to build your HTML designs with Less, and with greater ease, including the integration of Less into WordPress.

What you need for this book

To understand and fully profit from the contents of this book, we first expect you to build a website with CSS. A basic understanding of CSS will also be required. Understanding CSS selectors and CSS precedence will help you to get the most out of it. We will introduce these CSS aspects in short, in the first chapter. Understanding the basics of using functions and parameters in functional languages such as JavaScript is valuable but not required. Don't panic if you know nothing about functions and parameters, as this book contains clear examples. Even without any (functional) programming knowledge, you can learn Less and we will help you do this. The most important skill will be the willingness to learn.

All the chapters of this book contain examples and example code. Running and testing these examples will help you to develop your Less skills. You will need a modern web browser such as Google Chrome or Mozilla Firefox to run these examples. Use any preferred text or CSS editor to write your Less code.

Who this book is for

Every web designer who works with CSS and wants to spend more time on real design tasks should read this book. It doesn't matter whether you are a novice web designer or have used CSS for years, both will profit reading this book and learn Less. We also recommend this book for teachers and students in modern web design and computer science. Less does not depend on a platform, language, or CMS. If you use CSS, you can and should profit from Less.

Conventions

In this book, you will find a number of text styles that distinguish between different kinds of information. Here are some examples of these styles and an explanation of their meaning.

Code words in text, database table names, folder names, filenames, file extensions, pathnames, dummy URLs, user input, and Twitter handles are shown as follows: "Using the Less `autoprefix` plugin or the `-prefix-free` library will be the best practice to add vendor prefixes."

A block of code is set as follows:

```
.box-shadow(@style, @c) when (iscolor(@c)) {  box-shadow: @style
   @c;
}
.box-shadow(@style, @alpha: 50%) when (isnumber(@alpha)) {
   .box-shadow(@style, rgba(0, 0, 0, @alpha));
}
```

When we wish to draw your attention to a particular part of a code block, the relevant lines or items are set in bold:

```
#sidebar{
   h2{
      color: black;
      font-size: 16px;
      .screenreaders-only;
   }
}
```

Any command-line input or output is written as follows:

```
lessc --modify-var="mobile=true" source.less
```

New terms and **important words** are shown in bold. Words that you see on the screen, for example, in menus or dialog boxes, appear in the text like this: " In this case, the compiler throws an error: **RuntimeError: No matching definition was found for .mixin(a, b, c, d).**"

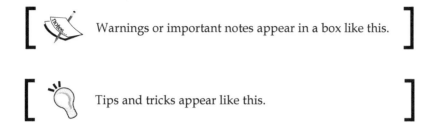

Warnings or important notes appear in a box like this.

Tips and tricks appear like this.

Reader feedback

Feedback from our readers is always welcome. Let us know what you think about this book—what you liked or disliked. Reader feedback is important for us as it helps us develop titles that you will really get the most out of.

To send us general feedback, simply e-mail feedback@packtpub.com, and mention the book's title in the subject of your message.

If there is a topic that you have expertise in and you are interested in either writing or contributing to a book, see our author guide at www.packtpub.com/authors.

Customer support

Now that you are the proud owner of a Packt book, we have a number of things to help you to get the most from your purchase.

Downloading the example code

You can download the example code files from your account at http://www.packtpub.com for all the Packt Publishing books you have purchased. If you purchased this book elsewhere, you can visit http://www.packtpub.com/support and register to have the files e-mailed directly to you.

Downloading the color images of this book

We also provide you with a PDF file that has color images of the screenshots/diagrams used in this book. The color images will help you better understand the changes in the output. You can download this file from http://www.packtpub.com/sites/default/files/downloads/4072OS_ColoredImages.pdf.

Errata

Although we have taken every care to ensure the accuracy of our content, mistakes do happen. If you find a mistake in one of our books—maybe a mistake in the text or the code—we would be grateful if you could report this to us. By doing so, you can save other readers from frustration and help us improve subsequent versions of this book. If you find any errata, please report them by visiting http://www.packtpub.com/submit-errata, selecting your book, clicking on the **Errata Submission Form** link, and entering the details of your errata. Once your errata are verified, your submission will be accepted and the errata will be uploaded to our website or added to any list of existing errata under the Errata section of that title.

To view the previously submitted errata, go to https://www.packtpub.com/books/content/support and enter the name of the book in the search field. The required information will appear under the **Errata** section.

Piracy

Piracy of copyrighted material on the Internet is an ongoing problem across all media. At Packt, we take the protection of our copyright and licenses very seriously. If you come across any illegal copies of our works in any form on the Internet, please provide us with the location address or website name immediately so that we can pursue a remedy.

Please contact us at copyright@packtpub.com with a link to the suspected pirated material.

We appreciate your help in protecting our authors and our ability to bring you valuable content.

Questions

If you have a problem with any aspect of this book, you can contact us at questions@packtpub.com, and we will do our best to address the problem.

1
Improving Web Development with Less

It is impossible to imagine modern web design without CSS. With CSS3, web designers are able to rely on advanced functions such as gradients, transitions, and animations. On the other hand, with these, the CSS code becomes more complex and difficult to maintain. Less is a CSS preprocessor that extends CSS with modern programming-language concepts. It enables you to use variables, functions, operations, and nesting (rule or selector) while coding your CSS. It also helps you write CSS with the **don't repeat yourself** (**DRY**) principle. The DRY principle prevents you from repeating any kind of information in your code.

This chapter will cover the following topics:

- Introduction to CSS3
- Compiling Less into CSS
- Vendor-specific rules
- CSS3 rounded corners, animations, and gradients
- Using box-sizing border-box
- Server-side compiling, setting up a build process, and using GUIs
- The OOCSS, SMACSS, and BEM methodologies

Using CSS3 for styling your HTML

In web design, you will use HTML to describe the structure of your documents and the CSS language to describe their presentation, including fonts, colors, and layout. The current standard HTML5 and CSS3 versions work on most modern browsers and mobile devices. CSS3 extends the old CSS with new selectors, text effects, background gradients, and animations. The power of CSS3, its new functionalities, and high acceptance on mobile devices using HTML5 and CSS3, makes it the standard for modern web design. The combination of HTML5 and CSS3 is ideal for building responsive websites because of their high acceptance on mobile phones and other devices.

Together, HTML5 and CSS3 introduce many new features. In this book, you will be shown and taught about the concepts of the most significant ones.

Using the CSS selectors to style your HTML

With Less (and CSS), you can style your HTML code using selectors. The CSS selectors are patterns or names that identify which HTML elements of the web page should be styled. The CSS selectors play an important role in writing the Less code.

For `body p.article {color:red}`, the selector here is `body p.article`. Selectors don't refer exclusively to one element. They can point to more than one element and different ones can refer to the same element. For instance, a single p selector refers to all the p elements, including the p elements with a `.article` class. In case of conflicts, cascade and specificity determine the styles that should be applied. When writing the Less code, we should keep the aforementioned rules in mind. Less makes it easier to write complex CSS without changing how your website looks. It doesn't introduce any limitations on your final CSS. With Less, you can edit well-structured code instead of changing the effect of the final CSS.

CSS3 introduces many new and handy selectors. One of them is `:nth-child(n)`, which makes it possible to style, for example, every fourth paragraph's p tag in an HTML document. The CSS code for the preceding description will look as follows:

```
p:nth-child(4n) {
  color:red;
}
```

Downloading the example code

You can download the example code files from your account at `http://www.packtpub.com` for all the Packt Publishing books you have purchased. If you purchased this book elsewhere, you can visit `http://www.packtpub.com/support` and register to have the files e-mailed directly to you.

Such selectors add powerful functions to CSS3. Nowadays, we are able to perform operations with CSS alone. However, in the past, we needed JavaScript or hardcoded styles (or classes at the very least). Less helps you organize and maintain these new selectors well and this is one of the reasons to learn it. Powerful selectors make CSS more important, but the CSS code also becomes cumbersome and difficult to maintain. Less will prevent this problem in CSS, even making complex code flexible and easy to maintain.

 Visit `http://www.w3.org/TR/selectors/#selectors` for a complete list of the CSS selectors.

Specificity, inheritance, and cascade in CSS

In most cases, many CSS styles can be applied on the same HTML element, but only one declaration for each individual property will win. The properties of an element may come from declarations in different rules. The W3C specifications describe the rules for which CSS styles will get the most precedence and will ultimately be applied. You can find these specifications in the next section.

The rules regarding the order of importance have not significantly changed with CSS3. They are briefly mentioned to help you understand some of the common pitfalls with Less/CSS and how to solve them. Sooner or later, you will be in a situation where you're trying to apply a CSS style to an element, but its effect stays invisible. You will reload, pull out your hair, and check for typos again and again, but nothing will help. This is because in most of these cases, your style will be overruled by another style that has a higher precedence.

The global rules for cascade in CSS are as follows:

- Find all the CSS declarations that apply to the element and property in question

- Inline styles have the highest precedence, except for `!important`.

    The `!important` statement in CSS is a keyword used to add weight to a declaration. The `!important` statement is added at the end of a CSS property value. After this, check who set the declaration; styles set by the author get a higher precedence than the styles defined by the user or browser (default). Author styles are defined by CSS in the web page; user styles are set by the user via the settings of his or her web browser; and default styles are set by the web browsers. The importance of the user is higher than the default, and the code with the `!important` statement (refer to *Chapter 2, Using Variables and Mixins*, for its meaning in Less) will always get the highest precedence.

Note that browsers such as Firefox have options to disable pages in order to use other alternatives to user-defined fonts. Here, the user settings overrule CSS of the web page. This way of overruling the page settings is not part of the CSS precedence unless they are set using `!important`.

- Calculate the specificity, which is discussed in the next section.
- If two or more rules have the same precedence and specificity, the one declared last wins.

As a Less/CSS designer, you will be making use of the calculated CSS specificity in most cases.

How CSS specificity works

Every CSS declaration gets a specificity, which will be calculated from the type of declaration and the selectors used in its declaration. Inline styles will always get the highest specificity and will always be applied (unless overwritten by the first two cascade rules). In practice, you should not use inline styles in many cases as it will break the DRY principle. It will also disable you from changing your styles only on a centralized location and will prevent you from using Less for styling.

An example of an inline style declaration is shown as follows:

```
<p style="color:#0000ff;">
```

After this, the number of IDs in the selector will be the next indicator to calculate specificity. The `#footer #leftcolumn {}` selector has two IDs, the `#footer {}` selector has one ID, and so on.

 Note that in this case, an ID is a unique selector starting with #. The `[id=]` selector for the same HTML element counts as an attribute. This means that `div#unique {}` has one ID and `div[id="unique"] {}` has zero IDs and one attribute.

If the number of IDs for two declarations is equal, the number of classes, pseudo classes, and attributes of the selector will be of importance. Classes start with a dot. For example, `.row` is a class. Pseudo classes, such as `:hover` and `:after`, start with a colon, and attributes, of course, are `href`, `alt`, `id`, and so on.

The `#footer a.alert:hover {}` selector scores two (one class and one pseudo class) and the `#footer div.right a.alert:hover {}` selector scores three (two classes and one pseudo class).

If this value is equal for both declarations, we can start counting the elements and pseudo elements. The pseudo elements are defined with a double colon (::) and allow authors to refer to otherwise inaccessible information, such as ::first-letter. The following example shows you how this works.

The #footer div a{} selector scores two (two elements) and the #footer div p a {} selector scores three (three elements).

You should now know what to do when your style isn't directly applied. In most cases, make your selector more specific to get your style applied. For instance, if #header p{} doesn't work, you can try adding a #header #subheader p{} ID, a #header p.head{} class, and so on.

When the cascade and !important rules do not give a conclusive answer, specificity calculation seems to be a difficult and time-consuming job. Although Less won't help you here, tools such as Firebug (and other developer tools) can make the specificity visible. An example using Firebug is shown in the following screenshot, where the selector with the highest specificity is displayed at the top of the screen and the overruled styles are struck out:

```
Inherited from ul.nav

.bs-sidenav {                                        docs.css (line 462)
    text-shadow: 0 1px 0 #FFFFFF;
}

.nav {                                         bootstrap.min.css (line 7)
    list-style: none outside none;
}

Inherited from body

body {                                         bootstrap.min.css (line 7)
    color: #333333;
    font-family: "Helvetica Neue",Helvetica,Arial,sans-serif;
    font-size: 14px;
    line-height: 1.42857;
}

Inherited from html

html {                                         bootstrap.min.css (line 7)
    font-size: 62.5%;
}

html {                                         bootstrap.min.css (line 7)
    font-family: sans-serif;
}
```

An example of specificity in Firebug

Building your layouts with flexible boxes

The **flexbox layout** (also called flexible boxes) is a new feature of CSS3. It is extremely useful in creating responsive and flexible layouts. Flexbox provides the ability to dynamically change the layout for different screen resolutions. It does not use floats and contains margins that do not collapse with their content. The latest versions of all major browsers, except from Opera mini, now support the flexbox layouts. Unfortunately, this support is not provided by many older browsers. Information about browser support can also be found at `http://caniuse.com/#feat=flexbox`.

We will focus on flexbox, due to its power. Also, as it is an important feature of CSS, we can also produce and maintain it using Less. You can access a set of Less mixins for CSS3 flexbox at `https://gist.github.com/bassjobsen/8068034`. You can use these mixins to create the flexbox layouts with Less, without using duplicate code.

These mixins will not be explained in great detail right now, but the following example shows how Less reduces the code needed to create a `flex` container. Using CSS, you might use the following code:

```
div#wrapper {
    display: -webkit-flex;
    display: -moz-flex;
    display: -ms-flexbox;
    display: -ms-flex;
    display: flex;
}
```

The preceding example uses the `.flex-display();` mixin to set the vendor prefixes for the `flex` value of the `display` property. In the *Vendor-specific rules* section, you will learn more about vendor prefixes and the Less `autoprefix` plugin. The Less `autoprefix` plugin makes it unnecessary to use vendor prefixes in your Less code. You can find the Less `autoprefix` plugin at `https://github.com/less/less-plugin-autoprefix`. Also, the `.flex-display();` mixin becomes unnecessary. Some ancient browsers use an older syntax for the flexbox layout, autoprefixing does not fix old syntaxes and polyfills.

The **flexbox grid** is a grid system based on the `flex` display property. This grid system can be used with the Bootstrap grid as a fall back for older browsers. The Less code to build the flexbox grid can be found at `https://github.com/bassjobsen/flexboxgrid` and the official website of the flexbox grid is `http://flexboxgrid.com/`.

Flexboxes have been mentioned because they have the potential to play an important role in the future of web design. In *Chapter 5, Integrating Less in Your Own Projects*, you can read about the flexboxgrid.com and flexible.gs grid systems, which are built with flexboxes. However, this book will mainly focus on creating responsive and flexible layouts with Less using the CSS media queries and the float property.

> Visit https://developer.mozilla.org/en-US/docs/Web/
> Guide/CSS/Flexible_boxes for additional information, examples,
> and browser compatibility.

Compiling Less

After delving into the theory of CSS, you can finally start using Less. As mentioned earlier, the syntax of Less is very similar to the syntax of CSS. More precisely, Less extends the CSS syntax. This means that any valid CSS code is, in fact, a valid Less code too. With Less, you can produce the CSS code that can be used to style your website. The process used to make CSS from Less is called **compiling**, where you can compile the Less code via server side or client side. The examples given in this book will make use of client-side compiling. Client side, in this context, means loading a Less file in the browser and using JavaScript on the client machine to compile and apply the resulting CSS. Client-side compiling is used in this book because it is the easiest way to get started, while still being good enough for developing your Less skills.

> It is important to note that the results from client-side compiling serve
> only demonstration purposes. For production, and especially when
> considering the performance of an application, it is recommended that
> you use server-side precompiling. Less bundles a compiler based on
> Node.js, and many other GUIs are available to precompile your code.
> These GUIs will be discussed toward the end of this chapter.

Getting started with Less

You can finally start using Less. The first thing you have to do is download Less from http://www.lesscss.org/. In this book, Version 2 of less.js will be used. After downloading it, an HTML5 document will be created. It will include less.js and your very first Less file. Instead of a local version of the less.js compiler, you include the latest version from a **content delivery network (CDN)**. Flexboxes have been mentioned because they have the potential to play an important role in the future of web design. For now, they are beyond the scope of this book. This book will focus on creating responsive and flexible layouts with Less using CSS media queries and grids.

The client-side examples in this book load from the `less.js` compiler CDN by using the following code in the section HEAD of the HTML files:

```
<script
    src="//cdnjs.cloudflare.com/ajax/libs/less.
js/2.x.x/
    less.min.js"></script>
```

Replace 2.x.x in the preceding code with the latest version available.

Note that you can download the examples from the support files for this chapter in the downloadable files for the book at `www.packtpub.com`.

Downloading the example code

You can download the example code files for all Packt Publishing books you have purchased from your account at `http://www.packtpub.com/`. If you purchased this book elsewhere, you can visit `http://www.packtpub.com/support/` and register to have the files e-mailed directly to you.

To start with, have a look at this plain yet well-structured HTML5 file:

```
<!doctype html>
<html lang="en">
  <head>
    <meta charset="utf-8">

    <title>Example code</title>
    <meta name="description" content="Example code">
    <meta name="author" content="Bass Jobsen">

    <link rel="stylesheet/less" type="text/css"
      href="less/styles.less" />
    <script
      src="//cdnjs.cloudflare.com/ajax/libs/less.js/2.2.0/
        less.min.js"></script>
  </head>

  <body>
    <h1>Less makes me Happy!</h1>
  </body>
</html>
```

As you can see, a Less file has been added to this document by using the following code:

```
<link rel="stylesheet/less" type="text/css"
  href="less/styles.less" />
```

When `rel="stylesheet/less"` is used, the code will be the same as for a style sheet. After the Less file, you can call `less.js` by using the following code:

```
<script
  src="//cdnjs.cloudflare.com/ajax/libs/less.js/2.2.0/
    less.min.js"></script>
```

Or alternatively, load a local file with a code that looks like the following:

```
<script src="js/less.js" type="text/javascript"></script>
```

In fact, that's all that you need to get started!

To keep things clear, `html5shiv` (which you can access at `http://code.google.com/p/html5shiv/`) and `Modernizr` (which you can access at `http://modernizr.com/`) have been ignored for now. These scripts add support and detect the new CSS3 and HTML5 features for older browsers such as IE7 and IE8. It is expected that you will be using a modern browser such as Mozilla Firefox, Google Chrome, or any version of Internet Explorer beyond IE8. These will offer full support of HTML5, CSS3, and media queries, which you will need when reading this book and doing the exercises.

> You already know that you should only use `less.js` for development and testing in most of the cases. There can still be use cases, which do justice to the client-side use of `less.js` in production. To support `less.js` for older browsers, you could try `es5-shim` (`https://github.com/es-shims/es5-shim/`).

Now open `http://localhost/index.html` in your browser. You will see the **Less makes me happy!** header text in its default font and color.

> It is not necessary to have a local web server running. Navigating to the `index.html` file on your hard drive with your browser should be enough. Or double click on the `index.html` file to open it in your default browser. Unfortunately, this won't work for all browsers, so use Mozilla Firefox in order to be sure. The examples in this book use `http://localhost/map/`, but this can be replaced with something similar to `file:///map/` or `c:\map\`, depending on your situation. Note that you cannot run `less.js` from CDN when using the file:// protocol in Google Chrome. You can not use the `less.js` compiler from CDN. You should replace it with a local version.

After this, you should open `less/styles.less` in your favorite text editor. The syntax of Less and CSS doesn't differ here, so you can enter the following code into this file:

```
h1{color:red;}
```

Following this, reload your browser. You will see the header text in red.

From the preceding code, `h1` is the selector that selects the HTML `H1` attribute in your HTML. The `color` property has been set to `red` between the accolades. The properties will then be applied onto your selectors, just like CSS does.

Using the watch function for automatic reloading

The `less.js` file has a `watch` function, which checks your files for changes and reloads your browser views when they are found. It is pretty simple to use. Execute the following steps:

1. Add `#!watch` after the URL you want to open, and then reload your browser.

2. Open `http://localhost/index.html#!watch` in your browser and start editing your Less files. Your browser will reflect your changes without having to reload.

3. Now, open `less/styles.less` in your text editor. In this file, write `h1{color:red;}`, and then save the file.

4. You should now navigate to your browser, which will show **Less makes me Happy!** in red.

5. Rearrange your screen in order to see both the text editor and browser together in the same window.

6. Furthermore, if you change `red` to `blue` in `less/styles.less`, you will see that the browser tracks these changes and shows **Less makes me Happy!** in blue, once the file is saved.

Pretty cool, isn't it?

> The preceding examples used color names instead of hexadecimal values. For instance, `red` instead of `#ff0000`. In this book, named colors are used throughout.

Debugging your code

As we are only human, we are prone to making mistakes or typos. It is important to be able to see what you did wrong and debug your code. If your Less file contains errors, it won't compile at all. So one small typo breaks the complete style of the document.

Debugging is also easy with `less.js`. To use debugging or allow `less.js` to display errors, you can add the following line of code to your `index.html` file:

```
<link rel="stylesheet/less" type="text/css"
  href="less/styles.less" />
<script type="text/javascript">var less = { env: 'development'
  };</script>
<script
  src="//cdnjs.cloudflare.com/ajax/libs/less.js/2.2.0/
    less.min.js"></script><script src="less.js"
      type="text/javascript"></script>
```

As you can see, the line with `var less = { env: 'development' };` is new here. This line contains `less` as a JavaScript variable used by `less.js`. In fact, this is a global Less object used to parse some settings to `less.js`. The only setting that will be used in this book is `env: 'development'`. For more settings, you can check `http://lesscss.org/#client-side-usage-browser-options`.

> The `env: 'development'` line also prevents Less from caching. Less doesn't cache files in the browser cache. Instead, files are cached in the browser's local storage. If env is set to `production`, this caching could yield unexpected results as the changed and saved files are not compiled.

Since Version 2 of Less, options can also be specified on the `script` tag, as shown in the following code:

```
<script src="less.js" data-env="development"></script>
```

Alternatively, you can use the `link` tag that refers to your source file, as follows:

```
<link data-env="development"' rel="stylesheet/less"
  type="text/css" href="less/styles.less">
```

To try this new setting, edit `less/styles.less` again and remove an accolade curly bracket to create an invalid syntax of the `h1{color:red` form, and then save the file.

In your browser, you will see a page like the following screenshot:

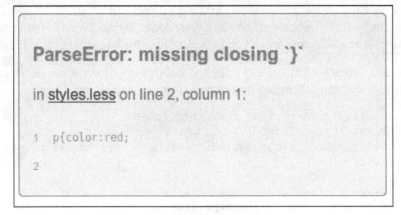

An example of a Less parse error

Besides syntax errors, there will also be name errors displayed. In the case of a name error, an undeclared function or variable would have been used.

It is possible to set other settings for debugging, either in the global Less object or by appending the setting to the URL. For example, you can specify the dumpLineNumbers setting by adding the following lines of code to your HTML file:

```
<script type="text/javascript">less = { env:
   'development',dumpLineNumbers: "mediaQuery"
};</script>
```

Alternatively, you can add !dumpLineNumbers:mediaQuery to the URL. You can, for instance, open http://localhost/index.html#!dumpLineNumbers:mediaQuery in your browser to enable the setting. This setting enables other tools to find the line number of the error in the Less source file. Setting this option to mediaQuery makes error reporting available for the Firebug or Chrome development tools.

Similarly, setting this to comments achieves the same for tools such as FireLESS. For instance, using FireLESS allows Firebug to display the original Less filename and the line number of CSS styles generated by Less. Older and experimental versions of Chrome did support this mediaQuery format. Currently, most browsers offer support for the CSS source maps, as described in the next section, in favor of other source mapping formats. The current version of Less does not support CSS sourcemap for in-browser usage. When developing in browser with the less.js compiler, you can use the FireLESS add-on for Firefox.

The `https://addons.mozilla.org/en-us/firefox/addon/firebug/` path shows that the Firebug add-on integrates with Firefox to put additional development tools, and the FireLESS add-on allows Firebug to display the original Less file name and line number of the Less-generated CSS styles. More information of using FireLESS with the latest version of Less can be found at `http://bassjobsen.weblogs.fm/fireless-less-v2/`.

Tools like Firebug, or the default Chrome browser development tools, or the default browser used to inspect the elements and functions of your webpage (which you can access by right-clicking on your browser screen) can also be used to see and evaluate the compiled CSS code. The CSS code is displayed as the inline CSS code wrapped inside a `<style type="text/css" id="less:book-less-styles">` tag. In the example given in the following screenshot, you will see an ID with the value `less:book-less-styles`. The values of this ID have been automatically generated by Less, based on the path and name of the `book/less/styles.less` Less file:

```
<style id="less:book-less-styles" type="text/css">
  1  p {
  2    color: navy;
  3  }
</style>
```

The Less-generated CSS styles

 If you set the `dumpLineNumbers` option to `comments` in the code shown in the preceding screenshot, you will see the file names and `linenumber` of the origin too.

Plugins

Plugins have been used since Version 2 of Less. They can be used with both the client-side and the server-side compiler. The current list of plugins can be found at `http://lesscss.org/usage/#plugins-list-of-less-plugins`. Writing a plugin yourself is not that difficult, but beyond the scope of this book. You can be sure that the list of useful plugins will grow over time. Less plugins described in this book only work in a node.js application (including Grunt and Gulp) and sometimes also for in browser usage.

The Less plugins can be grouped into the following four or five types:

- The first type, the so-called visitors, enable you to change the compile process. The inline URLs plugin converting `url()` to a call to `data-uri()` is an example of a visitor plugin.

- The second type are file manager plugins, which help you to set the files that should be compiled. Examples of file manager plugins are the npm import (https://github.com/less/less-plugin-npm-import) and bower resolve (https://github.com/Mercateo/less-plugin-bower-resolve) plugins.

- The post-process plugins form the third type. The autoprefix (https://github.com/less/less-plugin-autoprefix) and clean-css (https://github.com/less/less-plugin-clean-css) plugins are examples. They are able to change and modify the already compiled CSS code.

- The fourth type are the pre-process plugins. Pre-process plugins can automatically add the Less code before your custom code. You can use this type of plugin to load a complete library before your custom code. The Bootstrap plugin loads Bootstrap's Less code. You can find the Bootstrap plugin at https://github.com/bassjobsen/less-plugin-bootstrap.

- Finally, plugins can also be used to extend Less with your own custom functions. Plugins that extend Less with custom functions can be grouped in the fifth type, although these plugins, just like the visitor plugins, change the compile process. An example of a plugin, which extends Less with some custom functions, can be found at https://github.com/less/less-plugin-advanced-color-functions.

To use a plugin with Less in browser, you should first include the plugin source, and then set the plugin option of the less.js compiler. Your code will look like that shown in the following code snippet:

```
<script src="plugin.js"></script>
<script>
  var less = {
    env: "development",
    plugins: [Plugin]
  };
</script>
<script
  src="//cdnjs.cloudflare.com/ajax/libs/less.js/2.2.0/
    less.min.js"></script>
```

In this book, you will find many code examples. Unless explicitly mentioned, the format of these examples always shows the Less code first, followed by the compiled CSS code. For instance, you can write the following lines of code in Less:

```
mixin() {
  color: green;
}
```

```
p {
    .mixin();
}
```

This code will be compiled into the following CSS syntax:

```
p {
    color: green;
}
```

Your first layout in Less

You must first open `first.html` (from the downloadable files for the book) in your browser, and then open `less/first.less` in your text editor. In your browser, you will see a representation of a `header`, `body`, and `footer`.

As expected, `less/first.less` contains the Less code that will be converted into valid CSS by the `less.js` compiler. Any error in this file will stop the compiler and throws up an error message. Although the Less code shows some similarities to the plain CSS code, the process described here totally differs from editing your CSS directly.

The following screenshot shows you how this layout will look when opened in your web browser:

Your first layout in Less

Vendor-specific rules

CSS3 introduced vendor-specific rules, which offer you the possibility of writing some additional CSS applicable for only one browser. At first sight, this seems the exact opposite of what you want. What you want is a set of standards and practicalities that work the same with every browser, and a standard set of HTML and CSS that has the same effect and interpretation for every browser. Actually, these vendor-specific rules are intended to help us reach this utopia. Vendor-specific rules also provide us with early implementations of standard properties and alternative syntax. Last but not least, these rules allow browsers to implement proprietary CSS properties that would otherwise have no working standard (and may never actually become the standard).

For these reasons, vendor-specific rules play an important role in many new features of CSS3. For example, animation properties, border-radius, and box-shadow, depend on vendor-specific rules. You can easily see that some properties may evolve from vendor prefixes to standard. Currently, most browsers support the border-radius and box-shadow properties without any prefix.

Vendors use the following prefixes:

- **WebKit**: -webkit
- **Firefox**: -moz
- **Opera**: -o
- **Internet Explorer**: -ms

Autoprefixing

Vendor prefixes make writing the CSS code, and therefore the Less code, more complex. Also, you will have to change your code when your requirements change. In this book, you will find the code examples that use mixins for prefixing your CSS properties. Autoprefixing your code will be a better practice in many cases by consensus of the community. Examples of mixins used for prefixing can help you understand why mixins are easier to maintain and how they prevent code duplication. Even when you autoprefix your code, you will need mixins for non-standard code.

To autoprefix your code, you can use the Less autoprefix plugins. Note that you can read more about plugins in general in the *Server-side compiling* section.

With the `autoprefix` plugin, you can compile the following Less code:

```
#grad {
  background: linear-gradient(red, blue);
}
```

The preceding Less code compiles into the following CSS code:

```
#grad {
  background: -webkit-gradient(linear, left top, left bottom,
    from(red), to(blue));
  background: -webkit-linear-gradient(red, blue);
  background: -moz-linear-gradient(red, blue);
  background: -o-linear-gradient(red, blue);
  background: linear-gradient(red, blue);
}
```

The `autoprefix` plugin has got a browser's option. This option enables you to specify your target browsers. The Less `autoprefix` plugin is based on the autoprefixer plugin for PostCSS and gets its information about the browsers' features and usage statics from the **Can I use** (`http://caniuse.com/`) database. You can find the documentation for the Less plugin at `https://github.com/less/less-plugin-autoprefix`. The documentation of the Less plugin also refers to the `PostCSS` autoprefixer documentation to show you how to set your target browsers. The `PostCSS` autoprefixer, including documentation, can be found at `https://github.com/postcss/autoprefixer`.

Note that the autoprefixer only adds prefixes; adding `polyfill` or other alternative syntaxes is beyond the scope of the autoprefixer. Later on in this chapter, we will discuss how to create a background gradient. The background gradient code has an alternative fallback syntax for Internet Explorer 7 and 8. The autoprefixer does not add this alternative syntax to your CSS code.

In many situations, you can also consider a strategy of graceful degradation for older syntaxes. Graceful degradation means that you only add more user experience for modern browsers, without breaking the functionality of your design. One of the advantages of a graceful degradation strategy is that you do not have to try to run complex code on old and slow hardware, which can slow down your website. You can read more about graceful degradation at `http://www.w3.org/wiki/Graceful_degradation_versus_progressive_enhancement`.

The -prefix-free library

Unfortunately, the current version of the Less `autoprefix` plugin does not work when compiling your Less code in browser. The -prefix-free library offers an alternative for prefixing your code. The -prefix-free library runs client side in your browser and requires JavaScript. Client-side JavaScript can be a reason to not use it in production. The -prefix-free library only adds prefixes when needed, so it keeps your CSS as clean as possible. More information about -prefix-free can be found at `https://github.com/LeaVerou/prefixfree`.

To use `prefixfree.js`, you will just have to include `prefixfree.js` anywhere in your page. It is recommended to put it right after the style sheets, to minimize **Flash of unstyled content** (**FOUC**). FOUC means that your visitor sees your content before all styles have been loaded and applied. When you are using the -prefix-free library, your HTML should look as follows:

```
<link rel="stylesheet/less" type="text/css"
  href="less/project.less">

<script src="../../less.js" type="text/javascript"></script>
<script src="prefixfree.js"></script>
```

Build rounded corners with border-radius

The `border-radius` property is a new CSS3 property, which will make many web developers happy. With `border-radius`, you can give the HTML elements a rounded corner. In previous years, many implementations of rounded corners using images and transparency have been seen. However, these were inflexible (not fluid) and difficult to maintain.

Vendor-specific rules are required for implementation, so you will have to compile your code with the Less `autoprefix` plugin.

To give an element rounded corners with a radius of 10 pixels, you can use the CSS code with vendor-specific rules as follows:

```
-webkit-border-radius: 10px;
-moz-border-radius: 10px;
border-radius: 10px;
```

For rounded corners with different radii, use a list with values separated by spaces: `10px 5px 20px 15px;`. The radii are given in the following order: top-left, top-right, bottom-right, and bottom-left. By keeping these rules in mind, you will see how Less can keep your code clean.

You can open `roundedcornersbordered.html` from the download section of this chapter in your browser, and open `less/roundedcornersbordered.less` in your text editor. In your browser, you will see a representation of a `header`, `body`, and `footer` with a dark blue border and rounded corners.

The CSS code for `header` in `less/bordered.less` looks like the following code:

```
#header{
   background-color: red;
   border-radius: 10px;
   border: 5px solid darkblue;
}
```

You can see that the corners have been created with a radius of 10 pixels, set by the `border-radius` property, and the border itself has been set with the `border` property. If you were using CSS, you would have to repeat these properties three times for the `header`, `footer`, and `body`. In order to change these rules or add a vendor, you would also have to change the same code three times. To begin with, you might perhaps think, "Why not group the selectors?" in a fashion similar to the following code:

```
#header, #content, #footer{
   border-radius: 10px;
   border: 5px solid darkblue;-webkit-border-radius: 10px;
   -moz-border-radius: 10px;
   border-radius: 10px;
}
```

The preceding code is syntactically correct in order to write the CSS or Less code. However, as your code base grows, it won't be easy to maintain. Grouping selectors based on properties makes no sense when reading and maintaining your code. Moreover, such constructs will also introduce many duplicated and unstructured usages of the same selectors.

With Less, you are able to solve these problems efficiently. By creating a so-called mixin, you can solve the issues mentioned earlier. For the border radius, you can use the following code:

```
.bordered(@radius; @border-color) {
   border-radius: @radius;
   border: 5px solid @border-color;
}
```

To use the mixin mentioned in the preceding code, you should call it as a property for the selector, using the following code:

```
#header{
   background-color: red;
   bordered(10px, darkblue);
}
```

The compiled CSS of this Less code will now be as follows:

```
#header {
   background-color: red;
   border-radius: 10px;
   border: 5px solid darkblue;
}
```

Looking at the original code in the `less/bordered.less` file, you can see that the preceding code wouldn't be able to work for `#content`. The border radius for the content is 20 pixels instead of 10 pixels, as used for `header` and `footer`. Again, Less helps you solve this problem efficiently. Mixins can be called with parameters in the same way as functions can be called in functional programming. This means that in combination with a value and a reference for this value, mixins can be called in order to set the properties. In the following example, this will change to the following code:

```
.bordered(@radius: 10px; @border-color: darkblue) {
   border-radius: @radius;
   border: 5px solid @border-color;
}
```

In the `.bordered(@radius: 10px; @border-color: darkblue)` mixin, the `@radius` and `@border-color` variables are your parameters. The default value of the `@radius` parameter will be `10px` and the default value of the `@border-color` parameter will be `darkblue`.

From this point onwards, mixins can be used in your code. The `.bordered(50px);` statement will set the corners with a radius of `50px` and the `.bordered();` statement will do the same with a radius of `10px` and `darkblue` border color (default).

The same is true for the second `@border-color` parameter, which has a default value set to `darkblue`. A `.bordered(10px; white);` call will set a white border with a radius of `10px`. Note that Less supports both a comma and a semicolon as separator for the parameters of the mixins. Using commas can become confusing when your arguments are **comma-seperated values (CSV)**.

Using this, you can rewrite `less/borderedmixinsroundedcorners.less` so that it changes to the following code:

```
/* mixins */
.bordered(@radius: 10px; @border-color: darkblue;) {
  border-radius: @radius;
  border: 5px solid @border-color;
}
#header{
  background-color: red;
  .bordered();
}

#content{
  background-color: white;
  min-height: 300px;
  .bordered(20px);
}

#footer{
  background-color: navy;
  .bordered(10px; white);
}
```

The `less/roundedcornersborderedmixins.less` file, which is available in the download section, contains a copy of this code. To use this, you also have to change the reference in your HTML file to `<link rel="stylesheet/less" type="text/css" href="less/groundedcornersborderedmixins.less" />`.

 Note that this code leaves out the general styling of the `div` and body tags in HTML. These styles are only used to make the demo look good and do not actually demonstrate Less in any useful manner.

After rewriting your Less code, reload your browser or watch it if you have applied the `#!watch` trick. You will see that the output will be exactly the same. This shows you how to get the same results with Less, using a more efficiently structured code.

The preceding code will result into an example of a simple layout with borders and rounded corners. The final result should look like the following screenshot:

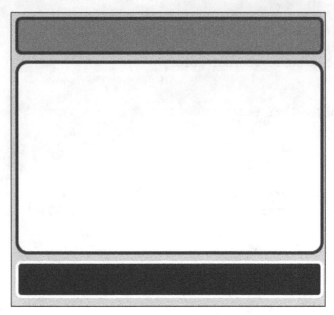

Layout with borders and rounded corners

Preventing cross-browser issues with CSS resets

When talking about cascade in CSS, there will definitely be a mention of the browser default settings getting a higher precedence than the author's preferred styling. When writing the Less code, you will overwrite the browser's default styling. In other words, anything that you do not define will be assigned a default styling, which is defined by the browser. This behavior plays a major role in many cross-browser issues. To prevent these sorts of problems, you can perform a CSS reset. The most famous browser reset is Eric and Meyer's Reset CSS (accessible at `http://meyerweb.com/eric/tools/css/reset/`).

The CSS reset overwrites the default styling rules of the browser and creates a starting point for styling. This starting point looks and acts the same on all (or most) browsers. In this book, `normalize.css` V2 is used. The `normalize.css` file is a modern, HTML5-ready alternative to the CSS resets and can be downloaded from `http://necolas.github.io/normalize.css/`. It lets browsers render all elements more consistently and makes them adhere to modern standards.

To use a CSS reset, you can make use of the `@import` directive of Less. With `@import`, you can include the other Less files in your main Less file. The syntax is `@import "{filename}";`. By default, the search path for the directives starts at the directory of the main file. Although setting alternative search paths is possible (by setting the path's variable of your Less environment), it will not be used in this book.

The examples of Less files in this book contain `@import "normalize.less";` in the first few lines of the code. Again, you should note that `normalize.less` does contain the CSS code. You should pay particular attention to the profits of this solution!

If you want to change or update the CSS reset, you will only have to replace one file. If you have to manage or build more than one project, which most of you may be doing, then you can simply reuse the complete reset code.

Creating background gradients

A new feature in CSS3 is the possibility of adding a gradient to the background color of an element. This acts as a replacement for complex code and image fallbacks.

It is possible to define different types of gradients and use two or more colors. In the following screenshot, you will see a background gradient of different colors:

A gradient example

The preceding example is taken from `http://www.w3schools.com/`.

In the next example, you can use a linear gradient of two colors. The background gradients use vendor-specific rules.

You can use the example code from the rounded corners example to add gradients to it.

The first step is to copy or open `less/gradient.less` and add a new mixin at the start of this file, as shown in the following code:

```
/* Mixin */
.gradient (@start: black, @stop: white,@origin: left) {
  background-color: @start;
```

```
    background-image: -webkit-linear-gradient(@origin, @start,
      @stop);
    background-image: -moz-linear-gradient(@origin, @start, @stop);
    background-image: -o-linear-gradient(@origin, @start, @stop);
    background-image: -ms-linear-gradient(@origin, @start, @stop);
    background-image: linear-gradient(@origin, @start, @stop);
  }
```

This will create gradients going from left (@origin) to right with colors from @start to @stop. This mixin has default values.

IE9 (and its earlier versions) do not support gradients. A fallback can be added by adding background-color: @start;, which will create a uniform colored background for older browsers.

After adding the mixin to your code, you can call on it for our #header, #body, and #footer selectors, as shown in the following code:

```
#header{
  background-color: red;
  .roundedcornersmixin();
  .gradient(red,lightred);
}
#content{
  background-color: white;
  min-height: 300px;
  .roundedcornersmixin(20px);
  .gradient();
}
#footer{
  background-color: navy;
  .roundedcornersmixin(20px);
  .gradient(navy,lightblue);
}
```

For example, if you renamed the Less file to less/gradient.less, you would also have had to change the reference in your HTML file to the following code:

```
<link rel="stylesheet/less" type="text/css"
  href="less/gradient.less" />
```

If you now load the HTML file in the browser, your results should be like the following screenshot:

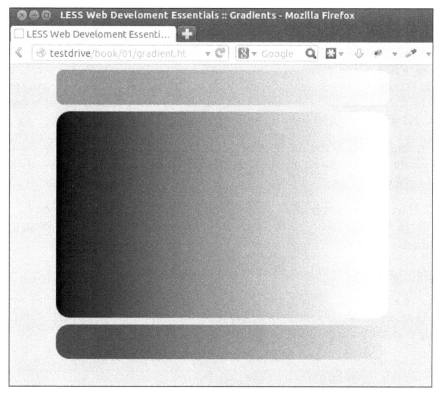

Gradients in the header, content, and footer from the example code

CSS transitions, transformations, and animations

Another new feature in CSS3 is the presence of transitions, transformations, and animations. These functions can replace the animated images, flash animations, and JavaScript codes in existing or new web pages. The difference between transitions, transformations, and animations isn't trivial. Animations are constructed with a range of `@keyframes`, where each `@keyframes` handles different states of your element in time. Transitions also describe the state of an element between the start and end of an event. They are mostly triggered by the CSS changes, such as a mouse over (hover) of an element.

To make things clear, it is important to keep in mind the button that is about to be pressed. The button will have two states: `pressed` and `not pressed`. Without transitions and animations, we are only able to style these states. The color of the button is white, but it becomes red when you hover the mouse over it. (In the CSS terms, its state becomes hovered by adding the `:hover` pseudo class.) In this case, the transition describes how the hovered button becomes red. For example, the change in color from white to red in two seconds (which makes it pink halfway) shows that the start of the color change is slow and changes faster as time passes. Using animations here enables us to describe the state of the button for every time interval between the start (not hovered) and end (hovered).

Transformations change the position of an element and how it looks. They do not depend on the state of the element. Some of the possible transformations are scaling, translating (moving), and rotating.

In practice, we use a combination of animations, transformations, and/or transitions in most situations. Also, in these cases, vendor-specific rules will play an important role.

Now a transformation will be added to our example.

Using the example code with rounded corners and gradients, copy the following code to `less/transition.less` or open `less/transition.less`, and add the following code to the beginning of the file:

```
/* Mixin */
.transition (@prop: all, @time: 1s, @ease: linear) {
  -webkit-transition: @prop @time @ease;
  -moz-transition: @prop @time @ease;
  -o-transition: @prop @time @ease;
  -ms-transition: @prop @time @ease;
  transition: @prop @time @ease;
}
```

This mixin example has three variables; the first is the property (`@prop`), which you will change. This can be `height`, `background-color`, `visibility`, and so on. The default value `all` shouldn't be used in the production code as this will have a negative effect on performance. The `@time` variable sets the duration in milliseconds or seconds with `ms` or `s` respectively appended to it. The last variable, `@ease`, sets the transition-timing-function property. This function describes the value of a property, given that a certain percentage of it has been completed. The transition-timing-function property describes the completeness of the transition as a function of time. Setting it to `linear` shows the effect with the same speed from start to end, while `ease` starts slow and ends slow, having a higher speed in the middle. The predefined functions are `ease`, `linear`, `ease-in`, `ease-out`, `ease-in-out`, `step-start`, and `step-end`.

Note that these mixins will not be needed when you compile your code with the Less `autoprefix` plugin. Similarly, the `.roundedcornersmixin();` mixin will not be needed and can be replaced with the `border-radius` property.

Now, you can edit `less/transition.less` to use this mixin. You can set the background color of the body when you hover over it. Note that you don't need to use the transition to change the gradient color but to rather change the `background-color` attribute. You are using `background-color` because `transition-duration` doesn't have a visible effect on the gradient. The code of the `background-color` transition is as follows:

```
#content{
   background-color: white;
   min-height: 300px;
   .roundedcornersmixin(20px);
   .transition(background-color,5s);
}
#content:hover{
   background-color: red;
}
```

If you renamed the Less file, for example, to `less/transition.less`, you would also have to change the reference in your HTML file to the following code:

```
<link rel="stylesheet/less" type="text/css"
href="less/transition.less" />
```

If you load the HTML file in the browser, you will be able to see the results there. Move your mouse over the content and see it change from white to red in five seconds.

Finally, a second example, that rotates the header, can be added. In this example, you will use `@keyframes`. Using `@keyframes` will be complex. So, in this case, you can define some vendor-specific rules and add these animation properties to `#header:` as follows:

```
@-moz-keyframes spin { 100% { -moz-transform: rotate(360deg); } }
@-webkit-keyframes spin { 100% { -webkit-transform:
   rotate(360deg); } }
@keyframes spin { 100% { -webkit-transform: rotate(360deg);
   transform:rotate(360deg); } }
#header{
   -webkit-animation:spin 4s linear infinite;
   -moz-animation:spin 4s linear infinite;
   animation:spin 4s linear infinite;
}
```

You can add the preceding code to our example files or open `less/keyframes.less`.

If you renamed the Less file, for example, to `less/keyframes.less`, you also have to change the reference in your HTML file to the following code:

```
<link rel="stylesheet/less" type="text/css"
  href="less/keyframes.less" />
```

Now, load the HTML file in the browser and watch your results. Amazing, isn't it? With a little bit of creative thinking, you will see the possibilities of creating a rotating windmill or a winking owl using only CSS3. However, the first thing that should be done is to explain the code used here in more detail. As mentioned earlier, there are many cases in which you would make combinations of animations and transformations. In this example, you also get to animate a transformation effect. To understand what is going on, we will split the code into three parts.

The first part is `@keyframes`, shown in the following code, which describes the value of the CSS properties (transformation in this case) as a function of the percentage of the animation completeness:

```
@keyframes spin { 100% { -webkit-transform: rotate(360deg);
  transform:rotate(360deg); } }
```

The name reference given to these keyframes definitions is `my-spin-effect`, which is not a special effect but only a chosen name. In the preceding example, a state of 100 percent completeness is described. At this state, the animated element should have made a rotation of 360 degrees.

This rotation is the second part that needs our attention. The transformation describes the position or dimensions of an element in the space. In the preceding example, the position is described by the number of degrees of rotation around the axis- 360 degrees at 100 percent, 180 degrees at 50 percent, 90 degrees at 25 percent, and so on.

The third part is the animation itself, described by the animation, `my-spin-effect`, which is `4s`, `linear`, and `infinite`. This is the shorthand notation of settings of the `sub` properties of the `animation` property. In fact, you can write this as the following code, without the vendor-specific rules:

```
animation-name: my-spin-effect;
animation-duration: 4s;
animation-timing-function:linear;
animation-iteration-count:  infinite;
```

You can use the three parts of the preceding code to build a complete animation. After doing this, you can extend it. For example, add an extra keyframe, which makes the time curve nonlinear, as follows:

```
@keyframes my-spin-effect {
  50% { transform: rotate(10deg);}
  100% {transform: rotate(360deg); }
}
```

You can add a second property using `background-color`. Don't forget to remove the gradient to see its effect. This is shown in the following code:

```
@-moz-keyframes my-spin-effect {
  50% { transform: rotate(10deg); background-color:green;}
  100% { transform: rotate(360deg); }
}
//.gradient(red,yellow);
```

You might have noticed that the complete profit of using Less isn't realized here. You will have to write the `@keyframes` definition repeatedly due to the different vendor prefixes its variable animation name. In *Chapter 4, Testing Your Code and Using Prebuilt Mixins Libraries*, a solution will be provided to you for this. Again, you can use the Less `autoprefix` plugin to solve this problem.

Unfortunately, browser support for transitions, transformations, and animations is not great and varies between browsers. Google Chrome does support CSS 3D transforms since Version 36. Older versions of Firefox lack support for the CSS filters, and IE9 (and earlier versions) don't support them at all. To solve this, many developers look to jQuery to support their animations. The `jQuery.animate()` function allows us to change the CSS properties of the elements using JavaScript. You can still use Less to set the initial CSS. An alternative for this would be to use `animate.css` (which you can access at `https://github.com/daneden/animate.css`); this cross-browser library of the CSS animations gets converted into the Less code with a jQuery fallback.

Box-sizing

The box-sizing property is the one that sets the CSS-box model used for calculating the dimensions of an element. In fact, box-sizing is not new in CSS, but nonetheless, switching your code to `box-sizing: border-box` will make your work a lot easier. When using the `border-box` settings, calculation of the width of an element includes border width and padding. So, changing the border of padding won't break your layouts. You can find a copy of the code used in this section in `boxsizing.html` from the download files.

Nowadays, most web designs use a grid. Grids split your design into columns of equal size. This helps you make things clear and build responsive interfaces. Depending on the available screen size (or width), you can show your content and navigation with a different representation of the same columns.

To handle different screen sizes, some parts of your website will have fluid width or height. Other elements, such as borders, gutters, and the white space, should have a fixed width. The combination of fluid widths as a percentage of the screen width (or viewport) with fixed widths becomes complex. This complexity will be due to the fact that browsers use different calculations for padding and margins of elements.

In order for you to see this, look at the following example. A container of 5300 pixels width has been created. Inside this container, you can add two rows and split the second row into two parts of 50 percent or half of its width.

```
<div class="wrapper" style="width:300px;">
  <div style="background-color:red;width;100%;">1</div>
  <div style="background-
    color:green;width:50%;float:left;">2</div>
  <div style="background-
    color:blue;width:50%;float:right;">3</div>
</div>
```

The output will now look like the following screenshot:

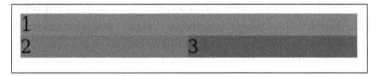

An HTML wrapper

The current structure doesn't show a problem until you add some padding, which is used to construct some space or a border between the two columns in the second row (numbers, **2** and **3**, in the screenshot of the HTML wrapper). The padding and the border will break our layout as follows:

```
<div class="wrapper" style="width:300px;">
  <div style="background-color:red;width:100%;">1</div>
  <div style="background-color:green;width:50%;float:left;
    border:5px solid yellow;">2</div>
  <div style="background-color:blue;width:50%;border:5px solid
    yellow;float:right;">3</div>
</div>
<br>
```

```
<div class="wrapper" style="width:300px;">
  <div style="background-color:red;width;100%;">1</div>
  <div style="background-color:green;float:left;width:50%;
    padding-right:5px;">
      <div style="background-color:yellow;">2</div></div>
  <div style="background-color:blue;width:50%;
    padding-right:5px;float:right;">3</div>
</div>
```

Finally, the output of this code should look like the following screenshot:

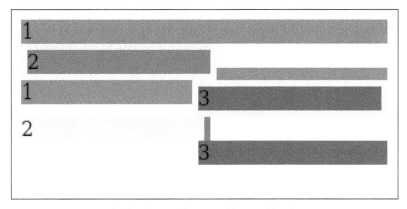

A broken layout due to padding and borders

A similar action can be performed, except that the wrappers can be wrapped inside an extra wrapper. The box-sizing: border-box; declaration can then be applied to this. Now, the results should look like the following screenshot:

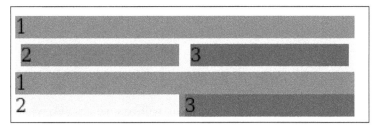

A layout with box-sizing: border-box

As you can see, the padding and borders are subtracted by 50 percent from the parent. This will make the calculation a lot easier. Of course, you can do the calculating yourself, once the parent container wrapper has a fixed width. If the parent has 300 pixels, 50 percent of this will be 150 pixels. Taking away the padding and the width of the border will give you the fixed size of a column. This won't work when your parent has a fluid width (the percentage of the viewport). Fluid layouts change their width with the width of the screen. If your screen becomes smaller, all the elements become smaller too and the percentage stays equal. You will quickly realize that doing calculations for all the possible screen sizes to find the real size of a column that allows all of your elements to align, is a long, challenging, and arduous process.

For these reasons, you should make use of `box-sizing: border-box;` for all the examples in this book. Note that `box-sizing` also has to be defined by vendor-specific rules, as follows:

```
-webkit-box-sizing: border-box;
-moz-box-sizing: border-box;
box-sizing: b/'order-box;
```

In this example, the Less code will be as follows:

```less
// Box sizing mixin
.box-sizing(@boxmodel) {
  -webkit-box-sizing: @boxmodel;
  -moz-box-sizing: @boxmodel;
  box-sizing: @boxmodel;
}
// Reset the box-sizing
*,
*:before,
*:after {
  .box-sizing(border-box);
}
```

 Note that the `.box-sizing` mixin will become obsolete when you compile your Less code with the Less `autoprefix` plugin.

With autoprefixing, your Less code can be reduced to the following code:

```
// Reset the box-sizing
*,
*:before,
*:after {
  box-sizing: border-box;
}
```

 The preceding code has been added into a separate file called `boxsizing.less`. From now on, the basics of our Less files will contain the following code:

```
@import: "normalize.less";@import: "boxsizing.less"
```

In the next chapters, you will learn more about organizing your Less code into files.

Server-side compiling

You have already taken the first few steps toward developing Less. As explained earlier, client-side compiling has been used. However, client-side compiling with `less.js` shouldn't be used on real websites. This is because, despite making your development easy and fast, compiling your Less files for every page request (or in fact, initial page load per user) will actually slow down your website.

For the production environment, it is required that you compile your files and serve the final CSS file to the browser. The term, server side, can be somewhat misleading. Server side in this context means that a compiled CSS code is sent to the client's browser instead of the Less code, which has to be compiled in the client's browser by `less.js` before it is shown. You should precompile your Less code. By copying and pasting the results of `less.js` to a file and including this as a CSS file in your HTML files, you should get the same effect, except that your CSS is not minimized.

Less bundles a command-line compiler. Installing and using it is simple, using the following command:

```
>> npm install -g less
>> lessc styles.less styles.css
```

Node enables you to run the JavaScripts without a browser. Node and npm run on Windows, Mac OS X, and other Unix/*nix machines. You will find the Node.js source code or a prebuilt installer for your platform by visiting http://nodejs.org/download/. The package manager for the Node JavaScript platform is npm. The npm command-line tool is bundled with Node.js, so installing Node.js will install npm at the same time. More information about npm can also be found at https://www.npmjs.com/package/npm.

Use the -help function to get a list of options you can use with the following command-line compiler:

```
>> lessc -help
```

The links to styles.css in your HTML, after successfully compiling it, are then shown as follows:

```
<link rel="stylesheet/css" type="text/css" href="styles.css">
```

Using CSS source maps for debugging

When working with the large Less code bases, finding the original source can become complex when viewing your result in the browsers. Since Version 1.5, Less offers support for the CSS source maps. The CSS source maps enable developer tools to map calls back to their location in original source files. This also works for compressed files. Both Chrome and Firefox developer tools support the CSS source maps format. Also, Internet Explorer Version 11 supports this format.

Currently, the CSS source maps debugging won't work for client-side compiling, as used for the examples in this book. However, the server-side lessc compiler can generate the useful CSS source maps.

After installing the lessc compiler, you can run the following command:

```
>> lessc -source-map=styles.css.map styles.less > styles.css
```

The preceding command will generate two files: styles.css.map and styles.css. The last line of styles.css now contains an extra line, which refers to the source map as follows:

```
/*# sourceMappingURL=boostrap.css.map */
```

In your HTML code, you only have to include the styles.css, as shown in the following code:

```
<link href="styles.css" rel="stylesheet">
```

When using the CSS source maps, as described in the preceding code, and inspecting your HTML code with Google Chrome **Developer Tools**, you will see something like the following screenshot:

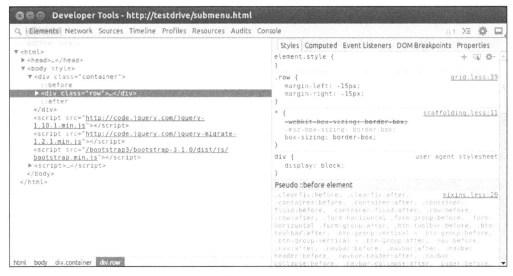

Inspect source with Google Chrome Developer Tools and source maps

As you can see, styles now have a reference to their original Less file, such as `grid.less`, including line number, which helps you in debugging. The `styles.css.map` file should be in the same directory as the `styles.css` file. You don't have to include your Less files in this directory too.

Plugins

The Less plugins can be installed with `npm` too. The `npm` plugin is the package manager for `Node.js`.

To install a Less plugin, you should run the following command on your console:

```
npm install less-plugin-{plugin-name}
```

To use an already installed plugin with the command-line compiler, you should use `plugin-name` as an option for the compiler. Options for the plugin can be set by leveraging the `=` sign, followed by the list of options.

Compressing and minimizing your CSS

After compilation, the CSS code is clean and readable. When taking this code into production, you have to compress and minimize it, in order to increase the loading speed and save on the bandwidth as well. The basic steps for compressing and minifying the CSS code are removing comments, whitespaces, and other unnecessary code. The results won't be easy for a human to read. However, this doesn't matter, because you can use the Less files to update or modify the CSS code.

The Less command-line compiler can compress the output when the `-comp ress` option has been set. This option removes whitespaces. More advanced minification can be done by using the `clean-css` postprocessor (which you can access at `https://github.com/GoalSmashers/clean-css`). Before Version 2, the compiler had `clean-css` built-in. Since Version 2, you have to install the `clean-css` plugin.

You can install the `clean-css` plugin by running the following command in the command line compiler:

```
npm install less-plugin-clean-css
```

After installing the plugin, you can run the compiler with the `–clean-css` option as follows:

```
lessc -clean-css file.less
```

With `clean-css`, refer to the following code:

```
.class1 {
  color: red;
}
.class2 {
  color: red;
}
```

The preceding code will compile into the CSS code, as the following code shows:

```
.class1,.class2{color:red}
```

As you can see, `clean-css` also merges the selectors. For advanced optimization of your code, which includes selector merging, you should run the `clean-css` plugin with the `advanced` option as follows:

```
lessc --clean-css="advanced" file.less
```

Also, **Pleeease** is a CSS post-processor, which can be used to run different post-process once. Pleeease, among others, runs the `autoprefixer` plugin, provides a fallback for the `em` units, and can merge media queries. A Pleeease plugin for Less is available, too.

You can read more about Pleeease at `http://pleeease.io/`.

Compiling your Less code into CSS automatically

When you are ready to start your first Less project, you should consider creating a build process that compiles your Less files into the CSS code automatically. Grunt and Gulp are task runners for `Node.js`. You can use these task runners to compile your Less code automatically and run postprocessors for the compiled CSS code.

The task runners can also be configured to detect file change and trigger browser reloads. Your final build system can show your changes directly after saving. Also, in the browser, development will be possible.

Gulp is relatively new in comparison to Grunt, so Grunt has more plugins and wider community support. Currently, the Gulp community is growing fast. The biggest difference between Grunt and Gulp is that Gulp does not save intermediary files, but pipes these files' content in memory to the next stream. A stream enables you to pass some data through a function, which will modify the data, and then pass the modified data to the next function. In many situations, Gulp requires less configuration settings, and so some people find Gulp more intuitive and easier to learn.

In this section, you will learn how to set up a build system with Gulp. Note that you can use the same strategies to do the same with Grunt. Those who are interested in build systems with Grunt can inspect the default build system of Bootstrap. You can read more about Bootstrap in *Chapter 6, Using the Bootstrap 3 Frontend Framework*. The Bootstrap source code contains a build system that compiles the code automatically leveraging Grunt.

To use Gulp, you should install `Node.js` first. As already mentioned, `npm` is bundled with `Node.js`. So, after installing `Node.js`, you can run the following commands in your working directory to install Gulp:

```
npm install -g gulp
npm install --save-dev gulp
```

The example code for this section can be found in the /gulp/ directory of the download for this chapter.

After installing Gulp, you have to create a Gulpfile.js file in your working directory. The Gulpfile.js file defines the task that it should perform on your files when running the gulp command. Your first Gulp file will look like that shown in the following code:

```
var gulp = require('gulp');
var less = require('gulp-less');

gulp.task('default', function () {
  gulp.src('./less/project.less')
  .pipe(less())
  .pipe(gulp.dest('./css'));
});
```

Now you can run the grunt command in the console, which will compile the Less code of the ./less/project.less into the ./css/project.css file. The basic build system uses the gulp-less plugin to compile your Less code. You can add more plugins such as gulp-sourcemap and gulp-autoprefixer in order to bring your build system to the next level.

The gulp-less plugin enables you to use the Less plugin, too. Using the Less plugins, instead of the gulp plugins, for tasks will simplify your Gulp configuration. You can use the task configuration shown in the following code to compile your Less code with sourcemaps, and the clean-css and autoprefixer postprocessors:

```
var gulp = require('gulp');
var less = require('gulp-less');
var sourcemaps = require('gulp-sourcemaps');
var LessPluginCleanCSS = require("less-plugin-clean-css"),
cleancss = new LessPluginCleanCSS({advanced: true});

var LessPluginAutoPrefix = require('less-plugin-autoprefix'),
autoprefix= new LessPluginAutoPrefix({browsers: ["last 2
  versions"]});

gulp.task('default', function () {
  gulp.src('./less/project.less')
  .pipe(sourcemaps.init())
  .pipe(less({
```

```
    plugins: [autoprefix, cleancss]
  }))
  .pipe(sourcemaps.write())
  .pipe(gulp.dest('./css'));
});
```

Finally, you can consider extending your build system with `gulp-livereload`. The `gulp-livereload` plugin can be used with the `livereload` Chrome extension. The `livereload` extension enables you to see the compiled version of your code in your browser directly after saving and opens the way to in browser development too. You can read more about `livereload` at `http://livereload.com/`.

Graphical user interfaces

Some of you will prefer to use a **Graphical User Interface** (GUI) instead of command-line compiling. There are many GUIs available for different platforms that can edit and compile your Less code. All of them cannot be mentioned here. Instead, here is a list of the most positive noticeable ones:

- **WinLess**: This GUI is a Windows GUI for `less.js`.
- **SimpLESS**: This GUI is a cross-platform editor and compiler with many functions, including the automatic addition of vendor-specific rules to your code.
- **CodeKIT**: This GUI is for Mac (OS X). It compiles many languages, including Less. It includes optimizations and browser previews.
- **Crunch!**: This GUI is a cross-platform compiler and editor.

When choosing a GUI for Less development, always check which version of `less.js` it uses. Some GUIs are built on older versions of `less.js` and don't support the latest features.

Web developers using Visual Studio should check out **Web Essentials**. Web Essentials extends Visual Studio with a lot of new features, including Less. Also, other IDEs such as PHPStorm have the built-in Less compilers. There is also a Less plugin for Eclipse.

The OOCSS, SMACSS, and BEM methodologies

As you already know, Less helps you write a reusable and more maintainable CSS. It also produces a valid CSS code, and features as the nesting of selectors already support you to keep related rules together. Less does not prescribe how to code your CSS. The **Object oriented CSS (OOCSS)**; **Scalable and Modular Architecture for CSS (SMACSS)**, which can be referred at https://smacss.com/; and **Block, Element, Modifier (BEM)**, which can be referred at https://en.bem.info/, methodologies discussed in this section will help you organize your Less code, resulting in well organized CSS too.

These methodologies work well together with Less. Now, we will discuss how to deploy them with Less.

All methodologies aim to split up your code into reusable blocks. Blocks should be independent of the design or page context, as far as possible. Most programmers will already be familiar with this kind of abstractions while for some designers, it will be a newer way of thinking. Imagine that you write down all style rules for the footer of your website in a separate file, and then you can reuse that file in a new project to style the footer again.

Most projects do not focus on only one methodology, but use concepts from different methodologies to build a strategy to organize the Less (or CSS) code. Also note that BEM, is, in fact, nothing more than a concrete application of OOCSS.

The focus of SMACC is the organizable structure of your code. SMACC code should be grouped into five categories: base, layout, modules, states, and theme. You can use the @import feature of Less to create a file structure for each group. When you inspect the Less code of projects such as Bootstrap, as discussed in *Chapter 6, Using the Bootstrap 3 Frontend Framework*, you will find that this code has also been organized in a similar way. You can read more about SMACC on the official website at https://smacss.com/. Most of the content of this website, the book, and the workshops are not available for free.

OOCSS focuses on the code structure of your code. With OOCSS, you will code reusable objects of styles. With OOCSS you work with reusable objects and each object contains styles rules for a HTML structure which holds a type of content. The basic rules of OOCSS help you to separate the structure from skin and container from content. The OOCSS media object is probably the most discussed example. You can read more about the media object at `http://www.stubbornella.org/content/2010/06/25/the-media-object-saves-hundreds-of-lines-of-code/`. When we create an object for buttons, it will look as shown in the following code:

```
.btn {}
.btn .btn-error{}
.btn .active {}
```

OOCSS not only tries to separate the container from the content, but also separates the style from the structure. In the button example, the `.btn` selector provides the structure while the `.btn-error` selector provides the styling. Also note that the `.btn .active {}` selector describes a state of your button object.

Nesting of selectors can be used to organize style rules for the button object together. The following Less code can be used for the button object:

```
.btn {
  .btn-error{}
  .active {}
}
```

As already mentioned, BEM is an application of OOCSS. The BEM syntax uses the following assumptions:

- CSS selectors are used to describe components (`.btn`)
- The selector name followed by __ (two underscores) and the descriptive name of the descendant are used for styling of the component (`.btn__btn-error{}`)
- Component's states can be declared by the name followed by - (double dashes) and the state (`.btnactive{}`)

The Less code for the button component using BEM will look like the following code:

```
.btn {
  &__error {}
  &--active{}
}
```

The preceding Less code makes use of the & parent selector and nesting, and will compile into the CSS code as follows:

```
.btn {}
.btn—error {}
. btn—active {}
```

Summary

In this chapter, you refreshed and extended your knowledge of CSS3. You learned how to compile your Less code on the client side. Furthermore, you wrote the code that allows you to have rounded corners, gradients, and animations in Less. You witnessed the profits of using Less and can now take the crucial initial steps to organize and plan your new projects. You also witnessed why you would want to use the CSS resets, how to compile these into the Less code, as well as how the box-sizing:border-box can make your job easier. You also saw what a mixin is, how to use it, and how you can import a Less file with the @import directive. You learned what is server-side compiling, how to set up a build process, and how to use GUIs. Last but not least, you got introduced to some methodologies that will help you to better organize your CSS code, leveraging Less.

In the next chapter, you will learn how to use variables in Less and how to build and use complex mixins.

2
Using Variables and Mixins

In this chapter, you will study Less in more detail, where you will learn more about variables and mixins. Variables in Less are often defined in a single place, but they can be used or overridden elsewhere in the code. In Less, you can override a variable by putting the definition afterwards. Variables are used to define commonly used values that can be edited only once at a single place. Based on the **Don't Repeat Yourself** (**DRY**) principle, commonly used values will help you build websites that are easier to maintain. Mixins are used to set the properties of a class. They bundle multiple declarations in a single line of code and are also reusable. You will learn how to create, use, and reuse them in your project and write better CSS without code duplications.

This chapter will cover the following topics:

- Using comments in Less
- Using variables
- Variable interpolation
- Escaping values
- Using mixins

Using comments in Less

Comments make your code clear and readable for others. It is important that you are able to understand them clearly. That is why this chapter starts with some notes and examples of comments.

Don't be sparse with your comments when keeping the file size, download time, and performance in mind. In the process of compiling and minimizing your final CSS code, comments and other layout structures will be effectively removed. You can add comments for understanding and readability wherever needed.

In Less, you can add comments in the same way as you did while writing the CSS code. Comment lines are placed between /* */. Less also allows single-line comments that start with //.

Using Less, only the true CSS comments (/* */) will be included in the generated CSS file. Minimizers will remove these comments in your final compiled style sheet. An example of this can be seen in the following code:

```
/* comments by Bass
.mixins() { ~"this mixin is commented out"; }
*/
```

Nested comments

Although Less, like PHP or JavaScript, doesn't allow nested comments, single-line comments that start with // are allowed and can be mixed with the normal comment syntax. This is shown in the following code snippet:

```
/*
//commented out
*/
```

Special comments

Minimizers define special comment syntax sometimes to allow an important comment, such as a license notice, to be included in the minimized output as well. You can use this syntax to write some copyright notices at the top of your style sheet. Using clean CSS and the default minimizer of the clean-css command-line compiler of Less, you should place this important command between /*! !*/, as shown in the following example code:

```
/*!
very important comment!
        !*/
```

Note that you should install the `clean-css` plugin before you use the `-clean-css` option. You can install this plugin by running the following command:

`npm install less-plugin-clean-css`

Using variables

Variables in Less help you to keep your files organized and easy to maintain. They allow you to specify widely used values in a single place and then allow you to reuse them throughout your Less code. The properties of the final style sheet can be set with variables. So, imagine that you don't have to search for every declaration of a specific color or value in your style sheets any more. How does all of this work? Variables will start with @ and have a name.

Examples of such variables include `@color`, `@size`, and `@tree`. To write the name of these variables, you are allowed to use any alphanumeric character, underscores, and dashes. This means that `@this-is-variable-name-with-35-chars` is a valid variable name.

Unfortunately, the use of @ is ambiguous in Less. As you have seen in the preceding chapter, parameters used by mixins also start with @. That's not all! As a valid CSS code is also a valid Less code, there will be CSS media query declarations that also start with @. The context will make it clear when @ is used to declare a variable. If the context is not clear enough, the meaning of the @ sign will be explicitly mentioned in this book.

You can give a variable a value, which will be called a declaration. A value can contain numbers, pixel values, strings, lists, and even complete rulesets. A ruleset assigned to a variable will be called a detached ruleset.

You can use a colon (:) to assign a value to a variable. A declaration ends with a semicolon (;). The following examples will make this clear:

```
@width: 10px;
@color: blue;
@list: a b c d;
@csv-list: a, b, c, d;
@escaped-value: ~"dark@{color}";
```

Since the release of Less version 1.7, you can also store groups of properties, nested rulesets, and media declarations, or even any other set of Less features in a variable. The code should be placed between brackets just like a mixin. We call this a detached ruleset.

You can find an example of a detached ruleset in the following code example:

```
@detached-ruleset: { color: white; font-size: small; };
```

The detached ruleset declared in the preceding example can be called as follows:

```
p {
  @detached-ruleset();
}
```

After the declaration of a variable, you can use the variable anywhere in your code to reference its value. This quality makes variables extremely powerful while programming the Less code.

Organizing your files

As you have seen, you only have to declare a variable once to use it anywhere in the code. So, to make changes to the variables, you also have to change them only once. The example code defines the variables in a separate file called `less/variables.less`. It is a great practice to organize your files. If you want to change something, you now know where to look.

If you recall the CSS resets and border-boxing properties from the preceding chapter, your main Less file will now look like the following code snippet:

```
@import "less/normalize.less";
@import "less/boxsizing.less";
@import "less/mixins.less";
@import "less/variables.less";
```

Here, the `@import` statement imports code from the file to the main Less file. Filenames are written between quotes and followed by a semicolon. Besides the Less files, you can also import the plain CSS files, which will not be processed for the Less directives; this will be explained in more detail in *Chapter 5, Integrating Less in Your Own Projects*.

Now, open `http://localhost/index.html` in your browser. You will see a straightforward website layout, which contains a header, content block, side menu, and three-columned footer, as shown in the following screenshot. All the layout items have blue accents. After this, open `less/variables.less` in your favorite text editor.

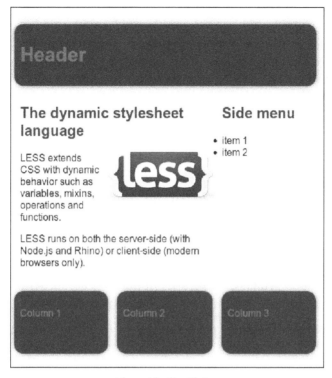

A layout built with Less

Curious as you are, you probably have also opened the other files already. Don't be scared by the complexity of the code in them. This code and layout has been used to show the power of widely-used variables that have been defined in a single place. This can be better demonstrated with more realistic and complex examples than by just a few lines of code. Rest assured that all the other code will explain this to you soon. Before you know it, all this code will look very familiar to you.

Firstly, change darkblue to darkgreen in the @darkcolor: darkgreen; line in the less/variables.less file, which you opened earlier. After this, watch the results in your browser. Reload your browser if you still haven't used the #!watch function.

The layout will now be shown in green. If you weren't convinced earlier, you should be now. In practice, you won't change a complete website using a single line of code, but this example shows what Less can do to make your work easier.

Imagine that you have finished your dark-green website's job and you show it to your boss. "Well done!" he says, but he also tells you, "I know I asked for green, but if you don't mind, I prefer a red website." For now, you smile and simply change darkgreen to darkred in the @darkcolor: darkgreen; line in the less/variables.less file.

As you have seen, your HTML is clean and straightforward with no inline CSS or even class names. There is now a new concern; you will have to name, declare, and save your variables in a smart and proper fashion. When doing this, be consistent and clear as it is of high importance. When organizing your variables, follow the same strategy at all times, using name conventions and comments where the context isn't clear enough. Keep in mind that someone should be able to take over your work without any further instructions at any moment. To achieve this, you will have to explore the variables at deeper levels.

Naming your variables

You should always give your variables meaningful and descriptive names. Variable names, such as `@a1` and `@a2`, will get compiled, but have not been chosen well. When the number of variable grows or when you have to change something quite deep in the code, you will not know or remember what `@a2` has been used for. You will have to look up its context to find its use in your Less files or even worse, inspect your HTML elements to find which CSS rules are applied on it in order to find the Less context. In this unfortunate case, you will be back to square one.

Good examples of names include `@nav-tabs-active-link-hover-border-color` and `@dark-color`. These variables are meaningful and descriptive because their names try to describe their function or usage rather than their value. This process of naming will also be called as `semantic naming`. So, in this case, `@dark-color` is a better choice than `@red`. Also, in some cases, you can be more specific by using `@brand-color`. This could describe some house style color of a website, as in the previous case. If the house style color changes from dark red to light green, `@brand-color: lightgreen;` still makes sense. However, `@dark-color: lightgreen;` or `@red: lightgreen;` just don't quite say it.

As you can see, hyphens are used to separate words in variable names. These names are called hyphenated names. You should use lowercase letters. There aren't any strict rules to use hyphenated names; the so-called **CamelCase** is used and is familiar to many programmers as an acceptable alternative. In CamelCase, you will use something similar to `@navTabsActiveLinkHoverBorderColor` and `@darkColor`. Both hyphenated and CamelCase names improve readability.

When writing the CSS and HTML code, you are probably already used to hyphening two-word terms, lowercase class names, IDs, and font names among other things. This book follows these conventions when writing the Less code and it therefore makes use of hyphenated and lowercase names.

Whether you prefer CamelCase or hyphenated names doesn't matter greatly. When you have chosen either CamelCase or hyphenated names, it is important to be consistent and use the same way of naming throughout your Less files.

 When you perform calculations, a hyphenated name may cause some trouble. You will need some extra spacing to solve this. When you declare @value minus one, @value-1 will be read as a single variable instead of @value -1.

Using a variable

If your project grows, it will be impossible to add a variable for every CSS property value, so you will have to choose which values should be a variable or which should not. There are no strict rules for this process. You will find some clear guidance to make these choices in the following sections.

You should first try to find the property values that are used more than once in your code. Repeated usage is suitable when creating variables. The @dark-color variable in the example code is a good example of such a property value.

Secondly, you can make variables of properties that are used for customization settings. The @basic-width variable in the example code is an example of such a property.

Finally, you should consider creating variables for reusable components. Looking at our example, you could reuse the header in other projects. To make this possible, you should create a new less/header.less file and import this to your main file with the following line of code:

```
@import "less/header.less";
```

Organizing variables

To make components reusable, you can create Less files for each component or function and arrange the variables to suit these files. To demonstrate this, split the example code into less/header.less, less/content.less, and less/footer.less.

The less/header.less file will now contain the following code:

```
header
{
  background-color: @header-dark-color;
  min-height: @header-height;
```

```
    padding: 10px;

    .center-content;
    .border-radius(15px);
    .box-shadow(0 0 10px, 70%);

    h1 {color: @header-light-color;}
}
```

Note that `@dark-color` has been renamed as `@header-dark-color`. Open `http://localhost/project.html` in your browser and `less/project.less` in the text editor to see all the changes and their effects.

Now, include `less/header.less` in `less/project.less` using `@import "header.less";` and create a `header` section in `less/variablesproject.less` as follows:

```
/* header */
@header-dark-color: @dark-color;
@header-light-color: @light-color;
@header-height: 75px;
```

The `@header-dark-color: @dark-color;` statement assigns the `@dark-color;` value to `@header-dark-color`. After this, you should do the same for `less/content.less` and `less/footer.less`. As you can see, `http://localhost/project.html` still looks the same after your changes.

Now, open `less/variablesproject.less` in your text editor and change the `footer` section to the one shown in the following code:

```
/* footer */
@footer-dark-color: darkgreen;
@footer-light-color: lightgreen;
@footer-height: 100px;
@footer-gutter: 10px;
```

In your browser, you will now see the layout with a green footer.

The last declaration wins!

In the preceding chapter, you read about the CSS cascade, where the last rule said that the value declared last will win if the output of the other rules is equal. Less uses the same strategy, where the last declaration of a variable will be used in all the preceding code. In this way, the Less variables are almost like constants in other languages. In the following code, you will see that the property value is set to 2 in accordance with the last declaration wins rule:

```
@value: 1;
.class{
  property: @value;
}
@value: 2;
Compiles into:
.class{
  property: 2;
}
```

In fact, Less first reads all of your code. When the value of a variable is used, it is only the last-assigned or last-read value that is actually used. The fact that the last declaration wins will only affect the declaration defined in the same scope.

In most programming languages, the scope is defined by a part of the code that the compiler can run independent of other code. Functions and classes can have their own scope. In Less, mixins have their own scope. Mixins will be discussed in more detail later on in this chapter.

The following code shows you that the property value is set to 3 in accordance with the value declared inside the scope of the mixin:

```
@value: 1;
.mixin(){
  @value: 3;
  property: @value;
}
.class{
  .mixin;
}
@value: 2;Compiles to:
.class{
  property: 3;
}
```

The preceding code means that you can't change variables during the compilation. This makes these variables theoretical constants. Compare this with a definition of the mathematical value of PI in your code, which is always the same. You will define PI only once, where PI = 3.14 will be in your code and will remain constant when your code is run. For this reason, variables should be declared only once when you want to use them as constants in your Less files.

Redeclaration of variables and the rule that the last declaration wins will be used in the customization of many Less projects and code.

To demonstrate redeclaration, create a new `less/customized.less` file and write the following code in it:

```
@import "styles.less";
@dark-color: black;
@basic-width: 940px;
```

Reference the `customized.less` file in the `customized.html` file as follows:

```
<link rel="stylesheet/less" type="text/css"
  href="less/customized.less" />
```

Now, load the `customized.html` file in your browser. As you see, you have created a customized version of your layout with only three lines of code!

Variable declaration is not static!

Although variables act like constants, their declaration is not necessarily unchangeable or static. First, you can assign a value of one variable to another, as shown in the following code:

```
@var2 : 1;
@var1 : @var2;
@var2 : 3;
```

The value of `@var1` is now 3 and not 1. Understand that you don't need to create some kind of reference as the rule, as the last declaration wins rule is applied here. The `@var1` variable will get the value of the last-declared `@var2` variable.

In the example code, you will also find the `@light-color: lighten(@dark-color,40%);` declaration. The `lighten()` function is a so-called built-in function of Less. *Chapter 3, Nested Rules, Operations, and Built-in Functions*, will cover the built-in functions. The use of the `lighten()` function sets `@light-color` to a calculated color value based on `@dark-color`. You should also pay attention to the last declaration of `@dark-color`, as this is used for color calculation.

Dynamic declaration of variable values gives flexibility, but keep in mind that you should only declare a value once and you can't change it after the declaration.

Lazy loading

Before you switch from variables to mixins, you should first know about lazy loading. In computer programming, this means to defer the initialization of an object until the point at which it is needed. Lazy loading is the opposite of eager loading. For Less, this means the variables are lazy loaded and do not have to be declared before they are actually used.

Trying to understand the theoretical aspects is all very well, but now, it is time to understand how they work in practice through the following example:

```
.class {
  property: @var;
}
@var: 2;
```

The preceding code gets compiled in the following code:

```
.class {
  property: 2;
}
```

Variable interpolation

In Less, variables can be used inside selector names, property names, URLs, and even import rules. The compiler applies string interpolation to replace the variable reference with its corresponding value.

Variables can be written with curly brackets around their name to prevent ambiguity. Take a look at the following Less code example:

```
@var: less;
.@{var} {
  property: ~"@{var}-5";
}
```

The preceding code will get compiled in CSS as follows:

```
.less {
  property: less-5;
}
```

Since Less v1.6, you can also use variable interpolation for properties. You can see this if you inspect the following Less code:

```
@property: width;
.fixed {
  @{property}: 100%;
  max-@{property}: 500px;
}
```

The preceding code will get compiled in CSS as follows:

```
.fixed {
  width: 100%;
  max-width: 500px;
}
```

In some situations, you will need quotes around the values; escaping these values will be explained in the next section. Variable interpolation can also be used to create `variable` variables, as can be seen in the following example:

```
@variable: red;
@color: "variable";
p {
  color: @@color;
}
```

The preceding code will get compiled in the CSS code, as follows:

```
p {
  color: red;
}
```

The usage of variable interpolation for variables has been limited to only one time; you cannot use the `@@@variable` code.

Escaping values

Less is an extension of CSS. This means that Less gives an error when you try to compile a CSS syntax that is not valid or uses a proprietary syntax, which Less doesn't recognize. Note that Less only checks the syntax and does not check whether the assigned value makes sense. The following code assigns a color to the `width` property:

```
p {
  width: darkblue;
}
```

Although the CSS syntax for the `width` property only allows `auto` | `value` | `initial` | `inherit`, with value the `width` value in px, cm, em, and so on, or a percentage assigned. Less also compiles the invalid color value.

Some browsers define properties with an invalid CSS code. Well-known examples will include some properties, such as `property: ms:somefunction()`. Some of these rules can be replaced by vendor-specific rules. It is important to note that the invalid property values won't get compiled in Less. To compile the `property: ms:somefunction()` value in your CSS code, you can use the following Less code:

```
selector {
property: ~"ms:somefunction()";
}
```

The preceding Less code gets compiled, without any error, in the CSS code, as follows:

```
selector {

  property: ms:somefunction();

}
```

The `~"ms:somefunction()"` code uses value escaping, which will be explained in more detail further in this chapter.

A new function, `calc()`, in CSS3 is a native CSS way of doing simple math as a replacement for a value of any length.

In both cases, Less won't give us the right value when we compile or import:

```
@aside-width: 80px;
.content {
  width: calc(100% -  @aside-width)
}
```

The preceding code gets compiled in the following code:

```
.content {
  width: calc(20%);
}
```

From the preceding code, `@aside-width: 80px;` is the declaration of a variable with the `aside-width` name. This variable gets a value of 80 pixels. More information on variables will be covered in the next sections. However now, more importantly, the preceding result is wrong (or at least, not as expected) because the `calc()` function should be evaluated during the rendering time. During the render time, the `calc()` function has the ability to mix units, such as percentages and pixels. In the preceding code, `.content` is assigned a width of `100%` of the available space (in other words, all of the available space) minus `80px` (pixels).

Escaping the values will prevent these problems. In Less, you can escape values by placing them between quotes (`""`) preceded by a tilde (`~`). So, in this example, you should write `width: ~"calc(100% -  @{aside-width})"`.

Note that the curly brackets are placed in the `aside-width` declaration's variable name, which is called a string interpolation, as discussed in the previous section. In the escaped values, anything between quotes is used as it is, with almost no changes. The only exceptions here are the string interpolated variables.

Strings are sequences of characters. In Less and CSS, values between quotes are strings. Without escaping, Less compiles its strings into the CSS strings.

For instance, `width: "calc(100 - 80px)"` doesn't make sense in CSS and neither does `width: calc(100% - @aside-width)`, because `@aside-width` has no meaning.

So, with escaping and string interpolation, you can start with the following code snippet:

```
@aside-width: 80px;
.content{
  width: ~"calc(100% - @{aside-width});"
}
```

The preceding code will get compiled in the following code:

```
.content {
  width: calc(100% - 80px);
```

 In the specific case of using the `calc()` function, the Less compiler has a `strict-math` option (used since version 1.4). This is used with `-strict-math=on` in the command line or `strictMath: true` when using JavaScript. When the `strict-math` option is turned on, the width of `calc(100% - @aside-width);` will get compiled into `width: calc(100% - 80px);`. Note that there have been many changes to this `strict-math` option during the development of the 1.6, 1.7, and 2.0 versions.

Using mixins

Mixins play an important role in Less. You saw mixins in the preceding chapter when the `rounded-corners` example was discussed. Mixins take their naming conventions from object-oriented programming. They look like functions in functional programming, but in fact, act like C macros. Mixins in Less allow you to embed all the properties of a class into another class by simply including the class name as one of its properties, as shown in the following code:

```
.mixin(){
  color: red;
  width: 300px;
  padding: 0 5px 10px 5px;
}
p{
  .mixin();
}
```

The preceding code will get compiled in the following code:

```
p{
  color: red;
  width: 300px;
  padding: 0 5px 10px 5px;
}
```

In the final CSS code used on the website, every `<p>` paragraph tag will be styled with the properties defined in the `mixin()` function. The advantage will be that you can apply the same mixin on different classes. As seen in the `rounded-corners` example, you only have to declare the properties once.

Try opening `less/mixins.less` from the available downloadable files of this chapter. In the examples of this book, all mixins are saved to a single file. In this file, you can arrange your mixins based on their functions. Grouping them in a single file prevents us from breaking the code while removing or replacing other functional Less files. Your project contains an example in `sidebar.less` and `content.less`, where both files make use of the `border-radius` mixin. If we now replace `sidebar.less`, you won't break `content.less`. Of course, you also don't want to have the same kind of mixins twice in your code.

The `box-sizing` mixin in `less/boxsizing.less` will be handled as a specific case. The `box-sizing` mixin influences all elements, and you can replace the `box-sizing` model in its entirety.

The `less/mixins.less` file contains four mixins, which will be discussed in the following sections. The `box-shadow` and `clearfix` mixins also have complex structures, such as nesting, but these mixins will be explained in further detail in the next chapter.

Basic mixins

You have seen the `rounded-corners` mixin already. A basic mixin looks like a class definition in CSS. Mixins are called inside classes and give these classes their properties.

In the example code in `less/mixins.less`, you will find the `.center-content` mixin, which sets the value of the `margin` property to `0 auto`. This mixin is used to center align the header, content wrapper, and footer.

 Note that these `center-content` mixins are not the one and only solution. A general wrapper to center align the header, content wrapper, and footer at once will also work for this example layout. The name of this mixin can also be discussed. When you decide not to center the content anymore, the name of this mixin will not make any sense.

Remove the `margin: 0 auto;` property, which in fact centers the content from the mixin. You should then reload `index.html` in your browser to see the effect.

Parametric mixins

As mentioned earlier, mixins act as functions in functional programming so, they can be parameterized as functions. A parameter is a value used in combination with mixins, with the parameter's name used as a reference to its value inside the mixin. The following code shows you an example of the usage of a parametric mixin:

```
.mixin(@parameter){
  property: @parameter;
}
.class1 {.mixin(10);}
.class2 {.mixin(20);}
```

The preceding code gets compiled in the following code:

```
.class1 {
  property: 10;
}
```

```
.class2 {
  property: 20;
}
```

The preceding example shows how parameterization makes mixins very powerful. They can be used and reused to set properties depending on the input values.

Default values

The parameters have an optional default value, which can be defined with `.mixins(@parameter:defaultvalue);`. To see how this works, you should consider the `border-radius` mixin in `less/mixins.less`, as shown in the following code:

```
.border-radius(@radius: 10px)
{
  -webkit-border-radius: @radius;
  -moz-border-radius: @radius;
  border-radius: @radius;
}
```

Note that the default value here is `10px`. When you call the preceding mixin without arguments, the default value will be used. Consider the following Less code:

```
div {
  border-radius(); // no arguments
  &.small {
    border-radius(5px);
  }
}
```

The preceding Less code gets compiled in the following CSS code:

```
div {

  -webkit-border-radius: 10px;

  -moz-border-radius: 10px;

  border-radius: 10px;

}

div.small {

  -webkit-border-radius: 5px;
```

```
    -moz-border-radius: 5px;

    border-radius: 5px;

}
```

Note that in the preceding example code, the `.small` class has been nested inside the `div` selector. The code also uses an `&` sign to reference the parent. You can read more about nested selectors and the `&` referencing sign in *Chapter 3, Nested Rules, Operations, and Built-in Functions.*

Naming and calling your mixins

In this book, mixins have meaningful and descriptive names and just like variable names, these names are hyphenated. Using meaningful and descriptive names for your mixins makes your code more readable for others and easier to maintain. Parameters and variables both start with an `@` sign. The context should make it clear whether it is a variable or mixin parameter that is being talked about.

To have a better understanding, consider the following code:

```
@defaulvalue-parameter1 :10;
.mixin(@parameter1: @defaulvalue-parameter1)
{
  property: @parameter1;
}
.class {
  .mixin
}
```

This code can be compiled in the following code:

```
.class{
  property: 10;
}
```

Note that `@defaulvalue-parameter1` is a variable here. The following code also illustrates the scope of a mixin:

```
@defaulvalue-parameter1 :10;
.mixin(@parameter1: @defaulvalue-parameter1){
  property: @parameter1;
}
.class {
```

```
    .mixin
}
  @parameter1 : 20;
```

This code can be compiled in the following code:

```
.class{
  property: 10;
}
```

Here, the last declaration of `@parameter1` is outside the scope of the mixin, so the property is still set to `10`.

Using mixins with multiple parameters

Multiple parameters for mixins can be separated by a comma or semicolon. Functional programmers often use a comma as a separator. In Less, a semicolon is preferred. A comma actually has an ambiguous role here, as they are not only used to separate parameters but also to separate list items in a list of **comma-separated values (csv)**.

The `.mixin(a,b,c,d)` call calls the mixin with four parameters. Similarly, the `.mixin(a;b;c;d)` call does the same. Now, consider the case where you call the mixin with the `.mixin(a,b,c;d)` call. Only two parameters are used here and the first parameter is a csv list of three items. If at least one semicolon is found in the parameter list, the only separator considered will be the semicolon. The following code shows you the effect of adding an extra semicolon to the parameter list:

```
.mixin(@list){
  property: @list;
}
.class{ .mixin(a,b,c,d;);}//see the extra semi-colon!
```

This code can be compiled in the following code:

```
.class{
  property: a, b, c, d;
}
```

Without this extra semicolon, you can call a mixin with four parameters. In this case, the compiler throws an error: **RuntimeError: No matching definition was found for .mixin(a, b, c, d)**. What you actually need is a mixin containing `.mixin(@a,@b,@c,@d)`.

The following Less code will give you an example of mixins "overloading", which means that the compiler compiles only the mixins that match the caller:

```less
.mixin(@color; @width) {
  border: 1px solid @color;
  width: 50px;
}
.mixin(@color;) {
  color: green;
}
p {
    &.onlycolor {
    .mixin(green);
  }
    &.including-border {
    .mixin(green;500px);
  }
}
```

The preceding Less code gets compiled in the CSS code, as follows:

```css
p.onlycolor {

  color: green;

}

p.including-border {

  border: 1px solid green;

  width: 50px;

}
```

In the preceding example, it has been made clear that mixins with the same name are allowed in Less. When finding different mixins with the same name, the compiler uses only the mixins with the right number of parameters or throws an error when no matching mixin is found. This form of parametric matching can be compared with method overloading, which is found in various programming languages.

If a mixin call matches more than one mixin, as shown in the following code, then all the matching mixins are used by the compiler:

```
.mixin(@a){
  property-a: @a;
}

.mixin(@b){
  property-b: @b;
}

class{
  .mixin(value);
}
```

This code gets compiled in the following code:

```
class {
  property-a: value;
  property-b: value;
}
```

More complex mixins for linear gradient backgrounds

You now have enough theoretical knowledge to build more complex mixins. In this example, you will add directive background gradients of three colors to the footer columns of our layout.

The final result should look like the following screenshot:

Linear gradient backgrounds built with Less

These gradient backgrounds have been chosen because of their complexity and well-documented changes over time. The final result will be a complex mixin, which is definitely not perfect, but improves the result significantly. You can be sure that you will have to change your gradient mixin from time to time because of the drop in support for old browsers, new browsers, changing specifications, and new insights. Refer to `https://developer.mozilla.org/en-US/docs/Web/Guide/CSS/Using_CSS_gradients` for some more examples.

You can't prevent these necessary changes, but you can minimize the time spent to keep your mixins up to date. Less guarantees that all of your background gradients are based on the same mixin defined in a single place.

At a basic level, background gradients in CSS are defined as images. For this reason, they are applied on the `background-image` property.

In this book, gradients are set on the `background-image` property. Other examples (elsewhere and perhaps in other books) will set them on the `background` property. There is no difference in their definitions. CSS defines different properties for backgrounds, such as `background-image`, `background-color`, `background-size`, and `background-position`. The `background` property is the shorthand for all of them together. When you define the first value of the `background` property as an image, or gradient in this case, all the other property values are set to their default value.

You can start your mixin by making a list of the following requirements:

- You want a parameter to set the direction of your gradient where you will use degrees
- Your gradient will consist of three colors
- After this, you can define a list of browsers and the browser version that you have to support

Now, you can define the first lines of your mixin, as follows:

```
.backgroundgradient(@deg: 0deg; @start-color: green; @between-
  color:yellow; @end-color: red; @between:50%)
{
  background-image: linear-gradient(@deg, @start-color, @between-
  color @between, @end-color);
}
```

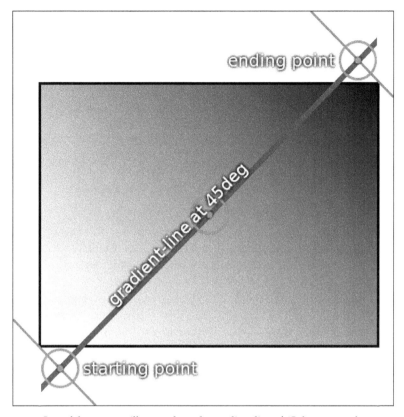

One of the ways to illustrate how the gradient line of 45 degrees works

The preceding image is taken from `http://dev.w3.org/csswg/css-images-3/`, Copyright 2013 W3C, 11 September 2013.

The background mixins have five parameters, which are as follows:

- The first parameter describes the direction in degrees. The number of degrees gives the angle between the vertical and the gradient direction. The description of the direction starts at the bottom. At the bottom, the angle is 0 degrees and describes a gradient from bottom to top. Then, the angle goes clockwise to 90 degrees point, which describes a gradient from left to right and so on.

- The next three parameters are the three colors of your gradient, which are the default values set for it.

- The fifth and last parameter defines where the middle color has its real value. The percentage here is a percentage of the width of the element that the gradient is applied on. The first and last color has `0` and `100` by default.

Modern browsers, such as IE version 11, Firefox version 16+, Opera version 12.10+, Safari version 7+, and Chrome version 26+ support these `background-image` properties. For older browsers, vendor-specific rules have to be added. The first problem here is that vendor-specific rules use a different way to define the angle. To compensate for this, you can use a correction of 90 degrees using the following code:

```
.backgroundgradient(@deg: 0deg; @start-color: green; @between-
  color:yellow; @end-color: red; @between:50%){
  @old-angle: @deg - 90deg;
  -ms-background-image: linear-gradient(@old-angle , @start-color,
    @between-color @between, @end-color);
  background-image: linear-gradient(@deg, @start-color, @between-
    color @between, @end-color);
}
```

The `-ms` background-image property is used by IE10, as an older version of IE is unable to support a background image. Alternatively, you can add a filter to support a two-color gradient. There is no support for using this filter in combination with a fallback image, so you will have to choose webkit-based browsers, such as Chrome and Safari, which use `-webkit-linear-gradient`. However, if you have to support older versions of these browsers, you will have to use `-webkit-gradient`. Note that `-webkit-gradient` has an unusual syntax. For example, your final mixin will look like the following code:

```
.backgroundgradient(@degrees: 0deg; @start-color: green; @between-
  color:yellow; @end-color: red; @between:50%){
  background-image: -moz-linear-gradient(@degrees, @start-color
    0%, @between-color @between, @end-color 100%);
  background: -webkit-gradient(linear, left top, left bottom,
    color-stop(0%, @start-color), color-stop(@between,@between-
      color), color-stop(100%,@end-color));
  background-image : -webkit-linear-gradient(@degrees, @start-
    color 0%, @between-color @between, @end-color 100%);
  background-image: -o-linear-gradient(@degrees, @start-color 0%,
    @between-color @between, @end-color 100%);
  background-image: -ms-linear-gradient(@degrees, @start-color 0%,
    @between-color @between, @end-color 100%);
  background-image: linear-gradient((@degrees - 90deg), @start-
    color 0%, @between-color @between, @end-color 100%);
  filter: progid:DXImageTransform.Microsoft.gradient(
    startColorstr='@startcolor',
      endColorstr='@endcolor',GradientType=0 );
}
```

The preceding code shows that even when using Less, our code can still be complex. Unless this complexity supports different browsers, you can see the advantage of using Less, which allows you to handle this code only once and at a single place.

The code in the preceding example can be found in `directivebackgrounds.html` and `less/directivebackgrounds.less`. If you wonder why you should use a CSS background gradient at all after all of this, take a look at `http://lea.verou.me/css3patterns/` and see what is possible.

In this book, it's argued that using the autoprefixer to prefix your code will be best practice. As already mentioned, the autoprefixer does not add nonstandard code nor polyfills to your CSS code. For nonstandard CSS code, using mixins seems the right way to go to build code that offers support for older browsers too. Mixins also make it possible to set background gradient with various parameters with the same code.

The @arguments and @rest special variables

Less defines two special variables. The `@arguments` variable is the first one and contains a list of all the arguments that are passed. The `@arguments` variable exists inside mixins. In Less, lists are defined separately with spaces, so you can use `@arguments` for properties that can be set by a list of values. Properties such as `margin` and `padding` accept lists in their shorthand notation, as shown in the following code:

```
.setmargin(@top:10px; @right:10px; @bottom: 10px; @left 10px;){
  margin: @arguments;
}
p{
  .setmargin();
}
```

This code can be compiled in the following code:

```
p {
  margin: 10px 10px 10px 10px;
}
```

The second special variable is `@rest variable`. The `@rest...` name binds all odd arguments after the preceding arguments from the caller to a list.

By doing this, `@rest...` gives us the opportunity to call a mixin with an endless argument list. Note that the three ending dots are part of the syntax.

The @rest... variable is just a name. In fact the ... syntax accepts the odd parameters and makes the mixin matching independent of the number of arguments. @rest... does the same, but the compiler assigns the odd parameters to an @rest variable. Instead of @rest..., you can also use @odd..., or any other name, with the only difference that the parameters are assigned to the @odd variable now.

The following code shows how @rest... binds all the odd parameters after the @a variable to the property2 property:

```
.mixin(@a,@rest...) {
  property1: @a;
  property 2: @rest;
}
element {
   .mixin(1;2;3;4);
}
```

This code will get compiled in the following code:

```
element {

  property1: 1;

  property2: 2 3 4;

}
```

You should also consider using @rest... as a csv list. To do this, you can rewrite the .backgroundgradient mixin from less/mixinswithdirectivebackgrounds.less to the following code:

```
.backgroundgradient(@deg: 0; @colors...) {
  background-repeat: repeat-x;


  background-image: linear-gradient(@deg, @colors);
}
```

Now, the mixin will accept an endless list of colors and you can use colors with the following code:

```
div#content {
  .backgroundgradient(
    0;blue,white,black,pink,purple,yellow,green,orange);
}
```

The following screenshot shows the result of the code using this background mixin:

Result of the .backgroundgradient mixin which accepts an endless list of colors now

Note that the `.backgroundgradient()` mixin does not set any vendor prefix. To support older browsers, you should compile this code with the Less `autoprefix` plugin.

Passing rulesets as arguments

Detached rulesets, as discussed in the *Using variables* section in this chapter, can also be used as an argument for a mixin. Detached rulesets as mixin arguments enable you to define mixins that wrap different rulesets in the same parent class or media query. The following Less example code shows you how to use this feature:

```
.large(@rules) {
  @media (min-width:960px){
    @rules();
  }
}

p {
  font-size: 1em;
  .large( {font-size: 2em;});
}

img.large {
  display:none;
  .large( {display:block; max-width:100%;});
}
```

You will find that the preceding Less code will get compiled in the CSS code, as follows:

```
p {

  font-size: 1em;

}
```

```less
@media (min-width: 960px) {

  p {

    font-size: 2em;

  }

}

img.large {

  display: none;

}

@media (min-width: 960px) {

  img.large {

    display: block;

    max-width: 100%;

  }

}
```

Also note that in the result of the preceding code, Less does not merge media queries. You can use the Less group CSS media query (npm install less-plugin-group-css-media-queries) or Less Pleeease (npm install less-plugin-pleeease) plugins to group the media queries in your compiled CSS code.

Return values

If you are used to functional programming or even know a mathematical function, you will expect mixins to have a return value. This simply means that you put x into it and get y back. Mixins don't have a return value, but you can mimic this behavior using their scope. A variable defined in a mixin will be copied to the scope of the caller unless the variable has been defined already in the caller's scope. The following example will make this clear:

```less
.returnmixin(){
  @par1: 5;
```

```
    @par2: 10;
}
.mixin(){
    @par2: 5; // protected for overwriting
    property1: @par1; // copied from returnmixin's scope
    property2: @par2;
    .returnmixin();
}

element{
    .mixin();
}
```

This code will get compiled in the following code:

```
element {
    property1: 5;
    property2: 5;
}
```

If you look at the preceding example, you can compare property2: @par2; with a function, such as property2 = returnmixin();.

> Using the scope to mimic a return value can also be applied on mixins. A mixin defined in another mixin can be used in the scope of the caller. However, these are not protected by the scope like variables are! This process is called unlocking. For now, unlocking is outside the scope of this book.

Changing the behavior of a mixin

To make mixins more flexible, it will be useful to influence their output based on their input parameters. Less offers different mechanisms in order to do this.

Switches

Imagine that you have a color(); mixin, which should set the color property to white or black depending on the context. Set the context with an @context: light; declaration and declare two mixins with the same name, as shown in the following code:

```
.color(light)
{
    color: white;
}
```

```
  }
.color(dark)
{
    color: black;
}
```

Now, you can use the `.color(@context);` mixin in your code, which sets the `color` property of your class to `white` or `black` depending on the value declared for `@context`. This may not seem useful now, but it will be useful within your growing project. Take a look at the Bootflat project at `http://www.flathemes.com/`. This project provides color variants of Twitter's Bootstrap. Twitter's Bootstrap is a CSS framework based on Less. Bootflat defines two styles where one style is based on the improved style of Bootstrap 3.0 and the other style is a Square UI style with the rounded corner removed. This project uses one switch to compile two different styles.

Argument matching

Less allows different mixins with the same name. If there are such mixins, every mixin that matches the caller's parameter list is used. Refer to the following `color` mixins:

```
.color(@color)
{
    color: @color;
}
.color(@color1,@color2)
{
    color: gray;
}
```

With the `color` mixins defined in the preceding code, `.color(white)` gets compiled in `color: white;` and `.color(white,black)` will give you `color: gray;`. Note that the `.color(white);` call doesn't match the `.color(@color1,@color2)` mixin, which needs two arguments and so, the compiler does not use this call.

Guarded mixins

Mixins of the same name with the same number of arguments are also possible in Less. All the matches are used in this case, as shown in the following example:

```
.color(@color){
    color: @color;
    display: block;
}
```

```
.color(@color) {
  color: blue;
}
.class{
  .color(white)
}
```

This code will be compiled in the following code:

```
.class{
  color: white;
  display: block;
  color: blue;
}
```

 Two declarations of color don't make sense in this case. Less doesn't filter out double declarations unless they are used in the exact same way.

Guards can be used to prevent trouble with double-defined mixins. A guard is defined with a keyword when it is followed by a condition. When the condition is true, a mixin is used. The following example makes things clear:

```
.mixin(@a) when (@<){
  color: white;
}
.mixin(@a) when (@>=1){
  color: black;
}
.class {
  .mixin(0);
}
.class2 {
  .mixin(1);
}
```

This code will be compiled in the following code:

```
.class {
  color: white;
}
.class2 {
  color: black;
}
```

Guards can be used as an `if` statement in programming. The comparison operators, such as >, >=, =, =<, and < can be used. One or more conditions can be combined in the same way when they are separated with commas, which evaluate as `true` if one of them is `true`.

The `and` keyword can be used to evaluate as `true` only when both the conditions are `true`, for instance, `when @a>1` and `@<5`. Finally, a condition can be negated with the `not` keyword, for instance, `when (not a = red)`.

 If you have used the CSS media queries earlier, you must realize that guards act in the very same way that a media query does in CSS.

Finally, guard conditions can also contain built-in functions. These functions will be discussed in the next chapter and act on all defined variables when they are not part of the argument list. The built-in functions of the guard conditions can be seen in the following code:

```
@style: light;
.mixin(@color) when iscolor(@color) and (@style = light) {
  color: pink;
}
.class() {
  .mixin(red);
}
```

This code can be compiled in the following code:

```
.class {
  color: pink;
}
```

In the case of `@style: dark;` or `.mixin(1);`, there was no match.

CSS guards

Since version 1.5, a guard can also be applied on the selector directly. The following example shows you how to apply guards directly:

```
h1 when (@mobile = true) {
  font-size: large;
}
```

The preceding code enables you to compile different versions of your CSS code from the same Less code source.

When you save the preceding Less code in a file called `source.less`, you can create two other Less files to compile your CSS, as follows:

```
mobile.less:
@import "source";
@mobile: true;
default.less:
@import "source";
@mobile: false;
```

Instead of creating different files, you can also leverage the `--modify-var` option of the compiler to compile your different versions of CSS. The `--modify-var` option enables you to override the already-defined variables in your code. As already discussed, Less uses lazy loading, which makes it possible to override a variable by putting the definition afterwards.

With a command-line compiler, you can compile a mobile version of your CSS code by running the following command in your console:

```
lessc --modify-var="mobile=true" source.less
```

While compiling your Less code in a browser, you can use the `modifyVars` option. The following line of HTML code sets the `modifyVars` option to `true`:

```
<link data-modify-vars='{ mobile: "true"}' rel="stylesheet/less"
    type="text/css" href="less/styles.less">
```

Using guards and argument matching to construct loops

When Less doesn't find a matching mixin, it goes to the next evaluation and doesn't break. This can be used in combination with guards and argument matching to construct loops. To show this, imagine 10 classes each containing a numbered background image. The `.class1` class has the `background-image` property value set to `background-1.png`; the `.class2` class has set the value of the `background-image` property to `background-2.png`, and so on, as seen in the following code:

```
.setbackground(@number) when (@number>0){
  .setbackground( @number - 1 );
  .class@{number} { background-image: ~"url(backgroundimage-
    @{number}.png)"; }
}
.setbackground(10);
```

This code can be compiled in the following code:

```
.class1 {
  background-image: url(backgroundimage-1.png);
}
.class2 {
  background-image: url(backgroundimage-2.png);
}
...
.class10 {
  background-image: url(backgroundimage-10.png);
}
```

The last mixin perhaps looks complex when you see it first, but if you try to evaluate the mixin yourself, you will see that it actually contains a lot of stuff you have learned before.

In the preceding code, the `setbackground` mixin calls itself. Programmers will call this a recursion. What happens here?

The `.setbackground(10);` call matches the `.setbackground(@number)` mixin when the condition is `@number>0`, so please make use of this. The first evaluation of `.setbackground( @number - 1 );` also matches the mixin. This means that the compiler runs the mixin again. This will repeat until `@number -1` is `0` and no matches can be found anymore. Now, the compiler will read ahead of where it stopped in order to use the mixin.

The last stop was at `@number = 1`, so the code evaluates the `.class@{number} { background-image: ~"url(backgroundimage-@{number}.png)"; }` declaration for the `@number = 1` condition. When the compilation stopped before, it was at `@number = 2`. So, it evaluates the `.class@{number} { background-image: ~"url(backgroundimage-@{number}.png)"; }` declaration for the `@number = 2` condition and so on. When we are back at `@number = 10`, all the code has been compiled. So, the compiler stops.

Besides guards and argument matching, the preceding example also contains an interpolated property in the `.class@{number}` class declaration as well as an example string interpolation with the escaping property when declaring the `~"url(backgroundimage-@{number}.png)";` code. Mixins also show the need to use an additional space while performing calculations. So, `@number - 1` won't be evaluated as one `@number-1` variable.

Using mixins to loop through a set of values

In some situations, you can define your value as a set of mixins and use that structure to create some repeating code. Consider the following Less code:

```less
.widths() {

  .set("small",100px);

  .set("medium",200px);

  .set("large",400px);

}


div {

  .widths();

  .set(@name,@width) {

    @classname: ~"@{name}";

    &.@{classname} {

      width: @width;

    }

  }

}
```

The preceding Less code will get compiled in CSS, as follows:

```css
div.small {

  width: 100px;

}

div.medium {

  width: 200px;
```

```
}

div.large {

    width: 400px;

}
```

The Less code used in this example is not easy to understand. The `.widths()` mixin withholds the `.set()` mixins calls, just like any other mixin will not output in the compile code directly. Inside the `div` selector, the `.widths()` call makes the `.set()` mixins available in the current scope. Then, the `.set()` mixins call the `.set(@ name, @width)` mixin in the same scope and each call uses the data set in the callers. The `&` symbol used in the mixin will be explained in the next chapter.

The `for` mixin library, which can be found at `https://github.com/seven-phases-max/less.curious/blob/master/articles/generic-for.md` also offers an alternative way to loop trough an array of values.

Leveraging the `for` structure, the preceding example can also be written as follows:

```
@data: "small" 100px, "medium" 200px, "large" 400px;

div {

  .for(@data); .-each(@width) {

    @classname: e(extract(@width,1));

    &.@{classname} {

      width: extract(@width,2);

    }

  }

}
```

The Less code example uses the `e()` and `extract()` built-in functions, which are described in the next chapter.

The !important keyword

The chapter ends with a note on the !important keyword in Less. Using !important in a declaration gives the declaration the highest precedence when two or more selectors match the same element. The !important keyword overrules inline styles, as shown in the following code:

```
<style>
  p{color:green !important;}
</style>
<p style="color:red;">green</p>
```

The preceding code will show the text in green. As the example shows you, you can use !important to change the styles, which you cannot edit, of the source with inline CSS. It can also be used to make sure a style is always applied. Nevertheless, please use !important with care, as the only way to overrule !important is to use another !important. Any incorrect or unnecessary use of !important in Less will make your code messy and difficult to maintain.

In Less, you cannot only use !important for properties, but you can also use it with mixins. When !important is set for a certain mixin, all the properties of this mixin will be declared with the !important keyword. This can be seen in the following code:

```
.mixin(){property1: 1;property2: 2;
}
.class{
  .mixin() !important;
}
```

This code will be compiled in the following code:

```
.class{
  property1: 1 !important;
  property2: 2 !important;
}
```

The !important statement can also be assigned to a variable, as follows:

```
@color: red !important;
div {
  color: @color;
}
```

The preceding Less code gets compiled in the CSS code, as follows:

```
div {
  color: red !important;
}
```

Summary

In this chapter, you learned about variables and mixins. You saw how defining variables and mixins at a single place will reduce your code and make it easy to maintain.

In the next chapter, you will learn more about mixins and how to nest and extend them. You will also read about the built-in functions of Less. Built-in functions can be used to manipulate values in mixins and other parts of your code.

3
Nested Rules, Operations, and Built-in Functions

In this chapter, you will learn how Less helps you organize your CSS selectors more intuitively, makes inheritance clear, and makes your style sheets shorter. You will also learn about operations and built-in functions. Operations let you add, subtract, divide, and multiply property values and colors. They also give you the power to create complex relationships between properties. You will also learn how to set variables or guards using the built-in functions in your Less code.

This chapter will cover the following topics:

- Nesting the CSS rules
- Using operations
- Using built-in functions in your code
- Using built-in functions in your mixins

The navigation structure

With the examples in this chapter, you will extend the layout from *Chapter 2*, *Using Variables and Mixins*, step by step with a navigation structure. You will build this navigation structure by styling an HTML list with Less. This navigation structure forms a menu in the sidebar of the layout.

The final result will look like the following screenshot:

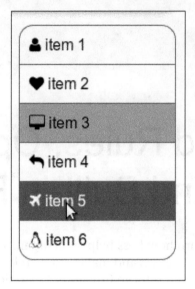

The final navigation menu built using Less

Working with nested rules

You will use the layout example from *Chapter 2, Using Variables and Mixins*, to study nesting of rules in more detail.

To do this, you must first open `http://localhost/index.html` in your browser, and then open `less/sidebar.less` in your text editor.

Anchors are added to the menu items. This means that the HTML of the side menu now looks like the following code:

```
<aside id="sidebar">
  <h2>Side menu</h2>
  <ul>
    <li><a href="page1.html">item 1</a></li>
    <li><a href="page2.html">item 1</a></li>
  </ul>
</aside>
```

You need a selector for each rule to style the different elements in CSS, as can be seen in the following code:

```
#sidebar h2{
  color: black;
  font-size: 16px;
}
#sidebar ul li a{
  text-decoration: none;
  color: green;
}
```

As you can see, both the `ul` (including the `li` element and the a anchor) and the `h2` elements are the children of the `aside` element with the `#sidebar` ID. CSS doesn't reflect this relationship because it is currently in the format as shown in the preceding code. Less will help you reflect this relationship in your code. In Less you can write the following code:

```
#sidebar{
  h2{
    color: black;
    font-size: 16px;
  }
  ul{
    li{
      a{
        text-decoration:
          none;
        color: green;
      }
    }
  }
}
```

The preceding code will compile straight into the following CSS syntax:

```
#sidebar h2 {
  color: black;
  font-size: 16px;
}
#sidebar ul li a {
  text-decoration: none;
  color: green;
}
```

The resulting CSS code of your compiled Less code is exactly the same as your original CSS code. In Less, you refer to the #sidebar ID only once, and due to the nesting of h2 and ul inside #sidemenu, your code structure is intuitive, and reflects the **Document Object Model (DOM)** structure of your HTML code.

To keep your code clean, a new less/sidebar.less file has been created. It contains the preceding Less code. Of course, this file should also be imported into less/ styles.less using the following line of code:

```
@import "sidebar.less";
```

Also, note that the sidebar is wrapped in a semantic HTML5 aside element instead of div element. Although this is more semantic, you will find that your sidebar has floated to the left after you have made these changes. To fix this, open less/ content.less in your text editor. By studying the nesting of the CSS selectors in the Less code, you will find aside float:right; nested in the .wrapper container. If you move this aside rule inside the #content container, the syntax will look like the following code:

```
#content {
  //two third of @basic-width
  width:(@basic-width * 2 / 3);
  float:left;
  min-height:200px;
  aside {
    float:right;
  }
}
```

In less/content.less, you will also find the line h2 { color: @content-dark-color; } line, which is in contrast to what you will see in the aside element. The h2 rule will still be overwritten by #sidebar h2{ color: black; }. The final rule contains a #sidebar selector, and so it has a higher CSS specificity, as explained in *Chapter 1, Improving Web Development with Less*.

Inspect the Less files, such as less/header.less, again and keep these brand new insights about nesting of the CSS selectors in mind. You will see that nesting is already used frequently. For example, in less/header.less, the properties of the h1 element are set by nesting.

A proper inspection of these files will also show you how mixins can be nested in classes and other mixins.

Although nesting of selectors is a useful feature of Less, you should use it with care. Nesting your selectors too deeply binds your DOM too tight to the CSS code, and also disables the possibility of overriding certain rules based on specificity.

Consider the following HTML snippet:

```
<header>
  <nav>
    <ul class="navigation">
      <li><a href="">Menu item 1</a></li>
      <li><a href="">Menu item 2</a></li>
    </ul>
  </nav>
</header>
```

The preceding snippet can be styled with the following Less code:

```
header {
  nav {
    ul {
      li {
        a {
          color: red;
          &:hover {
            color: green;
          }
        }
      }
    }
  }
}
```

In the situation that you, for instance, move the `nav` element into the `footer` element of your HTML document, the complete style will be broken. Also, overriding the green color of hovered links becomes more difficult, because you will need a long selector (`header nav ul li a:hover`) to create style rules with the same or higher specificity.

On the other hand, the nesting of the `&:hover` selector and the `a` element inside the `li` elements of the `nav` seems well thought out. These elements together form a navigation structure, and nesting helps to prevent collisions of styles. There is no golden rule that tells you how to apply the nesting of your selectors. Sometimes, people advise to restrict your nesting to a maximum of four levels deep. When your nesting becomes deeper than four levels, you should consider splitting your structure into smaller parts. For instance, if your design has got a footer with navigation, you can create a nesting for the basic elements and properties of the footer, and another one for the navigation. Consider the following Less code with a nesting of five levels deep:

```
footer {
color: green;
background-color: red;
  nav {
    ul {
      li { menu item
        li { // sub menu item


      }
    }
  }
}
```

The preceding code can be split as follows:

```
footer {
  color: green;
  background-color: red;
}
```

It can also be split in the following manner:

```
nav {
  ul {
    li { menu item
      li { // sub menu item
      }
    }
  }
}
```

The OOCSS, SMACSS, and BEM methodologies, described in *Chapter 1, Improving Web Development with Less,* will also help you to decide which selectors can be grouped together and nested.

Using mixins and classes

The name of a mixin should always end with parentheses; otherwise, it is a normal class. Mixins do not appear in your compiled CSS code, while classes do. Both mixins and classes can be nested in Less. Consider the difference in the following example Less code:

```
.class-1{
  property-1: a;
}
.class-2{
  .class-1;
  property-2: b;
}
```

This code gets compiled into the following code:

```
.class-1 {
  property-1: a;
}
.class-2 {
  property-1: a;
  property-2: b;
}
```

You can see how the properties of `.class-1` are copied into `.class-2` in the compiled CSS code. You add parentheses after `.class-1` in Less and make it a mixin. You should now consider the following code:

```
.mixin(){
  property-1: a;
}
.class-2{
  .mixin;
  property-2: b;
}
```

This code will get compiled into the following CSS code:

```
.class-2 {
  property-1: a;
  property-2: b;
}
```

Let's go back to the example of the side navigation menu. When your menu is ready, you will find that the navigating text inside the h2 heading element makes no sense. Unless you are visually impaired and use a screen reader, you can easily see that the side menu is intended as navigation for the website. So, you can hide this heading but should keep it visible for screen readers. Setting display:none will hide the element from the screen readers; visibility:hidden will also hide the element, but it still takes space and so can mess up your design. Setting the clip property will help in this situation. You can find more details at http://a11yproject.com/posts/how-to-hide-content/.

Based on the rule of precedence, you can write the following class using Less:

```
.screenreaders-only {
  clip: rect(1px, 1px, 1px, 1px);
  position: absolute;
  border:0;
}
```

Add the preceding class to less/boxsizing.less, and rename this file as less/basics.less. Also, don't forget to rename the import statement in less/styles.less. Now, you can use the following Less code to hide the h2 heading element in the sidebar menu:

```
#sidebar{
  h2{
    color: black;
    font-size: 16px;
    .screenreaders-only;
  }
}
```

After performing these steps and compiling the Less code into the CSS code, the sidebar navigation will look like the following screenshot:

- item 1
- item 2
- item 3
- item 4
- item 5
- item 6

A styled navigation menu with hidden heading text

As `.screenreaders-only` is a class and not a mixin, and classes are compiled into your final CSS code, not only can you use the `.screenreaders-only` class to add its properties to other classes in Less, but you can also use the class in your HTML code directly. This is shown in the following line of code:

```
<div class="screenreaders-only">Only readable for screen
  readers</div>
```

When working with Less, you will often have to choose between the specific compiled Less classes, based on your project's HTML structure, and a more generic solution that will be applied with a class inside your HTML code. Unfortunately, in these cases, there is no single solution. In general, DOM-specific code will generate more CSS code, but it will also keep your HTML code clean and give you the opportunity to generate more semantic HTML code. Reusing your Less code won't always be simple for this option.

Compiling your Less syntax as classes and using them in your HTML will make your code more reusable. On the other hand, it will mess up your HTML code. Also, the relationship between the CSS effects and the HTML structure becomes less strict. This makes it more difficult to maintain or change your code.

Variables

In `less/variables.less`, you should define a section for your sidebar, as shown in the following code:

```
/* side bar */
@header-color: black;
@header-font-size: 16px;
/* menu */
@menu-background-color: white;
@menu-font-color: green;
@menu-hover-background-color: darkgreen;
@menu-hover-font-color: white;
@menu-active-background-color: lightgreen;
@menu-active-font-color: white;
```

With the preceding variables, the Less code in `less/customsidebar.less` will now look like the following code:

```
#sidebar{
  h2{
    color: @header-color;
    font-size: @header-font-size;
```

```
    .screenreaders-only;
  }
  ul{
    li{
      a{
        text-decoration: none;
        color: @menu-font-color;
        background-color: @menu-background-color;
      }
    }
  }
}
```

Classes and namespaces

Before finishing the menu, the Less code used to style the menu will be changed to a class first. The points to consider here have already been discussed. A navigation is a general structure that can be used in many projects. In the class structure, it can be used to style any HTML list.

Create a new file for less/nav.less and write the following code into it:

```
.nav{
  li{
    a{
      text-decoration: none;
      color: @menu-font-color;
      background-color: @menu-background-color;
    }
  }
}
```

Now, you can turn every HTML list (ul or ol) in your HTML document into a navigation structure, just by adding the .nav class to it. This can be done using the following line of code:

```
<ul class="nav">
```

Note that with this Less code, lists can't be nested, and the items on the list should contain anchors (links). These requirements make it possible that this code can easily be (re)used in your other projects. Less also offers the possibility of defining namespaces. Namespaces can make your code more portable, and are defined in the same way as the CSS ID selectors. Namespaces start with a # symbol, as shown in the following code:

```
#lessnamespace {
  .nav {
    //code from less/nav.less here
  }
}
```

The #lessnamespace namespace can now be used as an example, as shown in the following code:

```
#sidebar {
  ul{
    #lessnamespace > .nav;
  }
}
```

In fact, a namespace doesn't differ from an ID selector. The #lessnamespace namespace can also be used directly in your HTML code, although this is not useful in most cases, as shown in the following code:

```
<div id="lessnamespace">
  <ul class="nav">
    ...
  </ul>
</div>
```

HTML requires every ID to be defined only once, so you can't repeat the use of the preceding HTML code in your HTML document, unless you append the ID to the body. Nevertheless, the preceding code shows that even the Less code written for a custom HTML DOM structure can be reused in other projects.

In the #lessnamespace namespace, as defined earlier, .nav is a class that makes direct usage possible. When .nav is changed to a mixin, it can only be reused in Less, as shown in the following code:

```
#namespace {
  .nav(){
    li{
      width:100%;
    }
```

```
    }
  }
#sidebar {
  ul{
    #namespace > .nav;
  }
}
```

This code will get compiled into the following code:

```
#sidebar ul li {
  width: 100%;
}
```

Referencing the parent selector with the & symbol

The & symbol plays a special and important role in Less as it references the parent of the current selector. You can use it to reverse the order of nesting, and to extend or merge classes. You will see that the following example will tell you more than what can be expressed in a thousand words:

```
.class1
{
  .class2{
    property: 5;
  }
}

.class1
{
  .class2 & {
    property: 5;
  }
}
```

This code will compile into the following code:

```
.class1 .class2 {
  property: 5;
}
.class2 .class1 {
  property: 5;
}
```

You can see that `.class2` becomes the parent of `.class1` when you use the `&` symbol after it. The `&` symbol can also be used to reference nesting that is outside the mixin, as can be seen in the example about the conditional `.ie8` class in the *Passing rulesets to mixins* section.

The `&` symbol can also be used to nest and append pseudo classes to a class. Later on, you will see that you can use it to append classes too. A simple example of this will be adding a `:hover` pseudo class triggered by a mouse hover to a link, as shown in the following code:

```
.hyperlink{
  color: blue;
  &:hover {
    color: red;
  }
}
```

This code can be compiled into the following code:

```
.hyperlink {
  color: blue;
}
.hyperlink:hover {
  color: red;
}
```

Now, open `less/mixins.less` in your text editor and find the `clearfix` mixin. The `clearfix` mixin uses the `&` symbol to append the `:hover`, `:after`, and `:before` pseudo classes to your elements, as shown in the following code:

```
.clearfix() {
  &:before,
  &:after {
    content: " "; /* 1 */
    display: table; /* 2 */
  }
  &:after {
    clear: both;
  }
}
```

With this new knowledge about the & symbol, it will now be easy for you to understand how to extend your example navigation menu with the :hover and :active (.active) states. The following code shows you how your extended code will look:

```less
.nav {
  li {
    a {
      text-decoration: none;
      color: @menu-font-color;
      &:hover {
        color:@menu-hover-font-color;
        background-color:@menu-hover-background-color;
      }

      width:100%;
      display: block;
      padding: 10px 0 10px 10px;
      border: 1px solid @menu-border-color;
      margin-top: -1px;// prevent double border
    }
    &.active {
      a {
        color:@menu-active-font-color;
        background-color:@menu-active-background-color;
      }
    }
    &:first-child a {
      border-radius: 15px 15px 0 0;
    }
    &:last-child a{
      border-radius: 0 0 15px 15px;
    }

  }

  list-style: none outside none;
  padding:0;
}
```

Open http://localhost/indexnav.html in your browser to inspect the results of the preceding syntax.

The extend pseudo class is a Less pseudo class, and uses the same syntax as a CSS pseudo class. The extend pseudo class adds the selector to the extended selector list. Adding the selector to the selector list of a different class gives the selector the same properties as the extended class. Remember the .hyperlink class in a previous example? If you extend this class, both classes will have the same properties.

```
.hyperlink{
  color: blue;
  &:hover {
    color: red;
  }
}
.other-
  hyperlink:extend
    (.hyperlink){};
```

This code will get compiled into the following code:

```
.hyperlink,
.other-hyperlink {
  color: blue;
}
.hyperlink:hover {
  color: red;
}
```

Note that the nested :hover pseudo class is not covered in .other-hyperlink. To extend a class, including the nested elements of the extended style, you will have to add the all keyword, as shown in the code in the following code:

```
.other-
  hyperlink:extend
    (.hyperlink all){};
```

This code now gets compiled into the following code:

```
.hyperlink,
.other-hyperlink {
  color: blue;
}
.hyperlink:hover,
.other-hyperlink:hover {
  color: red;
}
```

In cases where you nest the `:extend` statement, you have to use the `&` symbol as a reference, as shown in the following code:

```
.other-hyperlink{
    &:extend(.hyperlink);
};
```

In spite of the fact that the `extend` syntax mimics the syntax of the pseudo class, both of them can be combined, as long as `:extend` is added at the end of the selector. This is shown in the following code:

```
.other-hyperlink:hover:extend(.hyperlink){};
```

In summary, the `extend` syntax allows you to inherit a set of static properties from one ruleset to another. You can still augment the inherited ruleset with with your own rules. Consider the code in `less/customsidebar.less` again. You can use the `extend` feature to style a second sidebar with a different background color. The Less code for your second sidebar will look like the following code; you can find a copy of this code in `less/second-sidebar.less` of the downloads:

```
@import (reference) "basics";
@import (reference) "mixins";
@import (reference) "variables";
@import (reference) "customsidebar";

.second-sidebar {
    &:extend( #sidebar all);
    ul li a {
        background-color: green;
    }
}
```

The preceding Less code will compile in the following CSS code:

```
.second-sidebar h2 {
    color: black;
    font-size: 16px;
    clip: rect(1px, 1px, 1px, 1px);
    position: absolute;
    border: 0;
}

.second-sidebar ul li a {
    text-decoration: none;
    color: green;
```

```
    background-color: white;
  }

  .second-sidebar ul li a {
    background-color: green;
  }
```

When you only have to inherent a set of static CSS properties using the `extend` syntax instead of mixins, it will result in more compact (and therefore efficient) CSS code. On the other hand, mixins are more flexible as they can be paramized.

Guards nesting and the & usage

In *Chapter 2, Using Variables and Mixins*, you learned about guards. You can use guards along with the & symbol to construct some kind of if-else(-then). Consider the following Less code to see how this usage works:

```
.color(@number) {
  & when (@number>5) {
    color: red;
  }
  & when (@number<=5){
    color:green;
  }
}
p {
  .color(6);
}
p {
  .color(1);
}
```

The preceding Less code compiles into CSS code as follows:

```
p {
  color: red;
}
p {
  color: green;
}
```

Passing rulesets to mixins

In *Chapter 2, Using Variables and Mixins,* you read about the parametric mixins. Since the 1.7.0 release of Less, you can also use a so-called detached ruleset as an argument for a mixin. Detached rulesets can be stored in a variable and can contain any valid Less code such as grouped selectors, nested rulesets, media declarations, and built-in functions.

Detached rules can be called by appending parentheses after their names. The content of the detached ruleset has been copied to the position of the caller.

An example of a detached ruleset can be found in the following Less code:

```
@color-ruleset: { color: red; };
p {
  @color-ruleset();
}
```

The preceding code will compile into the CSS code as follows:

```
p {
  color: red;
}
```

Mixins with detached rules can be used to prevent code duplication in case you need different style rules for different media queries or classes. Consider the following Less code to get a grip on this useful usage of Less' detached rules feature.

```
.smallscreens(@rules){
  @media(max-width:767px) {
    @rules();
  }
}

.widescreens(@rules){
  @media(min-width:768px) {
    @rules();
  }
}
article {
  .smallscreens({width:100%; float:none; font-size:1em;});
  .widecreens({width:50%; float:left; font-size:1.5em;});
}
```

The technique of using detached rules, as described in the preceding code, can also be used with the conditional `<html>` classes. The conditional `<html>` classes are introduced as an alternative for conditional style sheets in the article, *Conditional Stylesheets vs CSS Hacks? Answer: Neither!, Paul Irish*. This article can be found at `http://www.paulirish.com/2008/conditional-stylesheets-vs-css-hacks-answer-neither/`. Modernizr is a feature detection library for HTML5/CSS3. Also, modernizr adds additional classes to the `<html>` tag for detected features. Modernizr can be found at `http://modernizr.com/`.

Consider the following example code, which sets a `red` background color for the `header` loop for the browser's target by the conditional `ie8` class:

```
.oldbrowsers(@rules) {
  .ie8 & {
    @rules();
  }
}
header {
  background-color: green;
  .oldbrowsers
    ({background-color:red;});
}
```

The preceding Less code will compile into the following CSS code:

```
header {
  background-color: green;
}

.ie8 header {
  background-color: red;
}
```

In the preceding code, the `&` sign in the `.ie8 &` selector is a reference to the parent of the caller of the `.oldbrowsers()` mixin.

Operating on numbers, colors, and variables

Less has a support for the basic arithmetic operations: addition (+), subtraction (-), multiplication (*), and division (/). In the `strict-math` mode, operations should be placed between parentheses. You can apply an operation on variables, values, and numbers. These operations help you make relationships between variables.

Open `less/footer.less` to immediately see the operation that you used, as in the following code, and its benefits:

```
footer {
  div {
    float: left;
    width: ((@basic-width / 3 ) - @footer-gutter);
  }
}
```

In the preceding code, the / sign (division) has been used to give the `footer` columns one-third of the available width (as set by `@basic-width`). Using operations in your code feels so natural that you may not even have realized that you have been using them until now. Less uses normal order precedence, where you can add extra parentheses to explicitly set precedence and avoid confusion. For instance, in Less, 3 + 3 * 3 gives 12. So, (3 + 3) * 3 equals 18, as shown in the following code:

```
.mixin(){
  property1: (3 + 3 * 3);
  property2: ((3 + 3) * 3);
}
.class {
  .mixin;
}
```

This code will get compiled into the following code:

```
.class {
  property1: 12;
  property2: 18;
}
```

The Less operations can also be used for color manipulation, and operations can be applied to values and colors with different units, as shown in the following code:

```
@color: yellow;
.mixin(){
  property1: (100px * 4);
  property2: (6% * 1px);
  property3: (#ffffff -
    #111111);
  property4: (@color / 10%)
}
.class {
  .mixin;
}
```

This code will get compiled into the following code:

```
.class {
  property1: 400px;
  property2: 6%;
  property3: #eeeeee;
  property4: #1a1a00;
}
```

Property merging

Property merging is useful if properties accept a **comma-separated value (CSV)** or space-separated lists. You will find this type of property mostly in CSS3, where borders, backgrounds, and transitions accept a CSV list. However, you will also find that the old-school `font-family` parameter accepts a list of font names that are separated by commas. Properties are merged by adding a + flag for comma-separated lists, or a +_ flag for space-separated lists, after their names. The following code will show you how to merge values with a comma:

```
.alternative-font()
{
  font-family+: Georgia,Serif;
}
.font()
{
  font-family+: Arial;
  .alternative-font;
}
body {
  .font;
}
```

This code will get compiled into the following code:

```
body {
  font-family: Arial, Georgia,Serif;
}
```

For space-separated lists, you can consider the following Less code:

```
.text-overflow(@text-overflow: ellipsis) {
  text-overflow+_ : @text-overflow;
}
p, .text-overflow {
  .text-overflow();
  text-overflow+_ : ellipsis;
}
```

The compiled CSS code of the preceding Less code will look as follows:

```
p,
.text-overflow {
  text-overflow: ellipsis ellipsis;
}
```

Built-in functions

Less supports many handy built-in functions. A built-in function can be used to manipulate the Less values inside mixins and set the variables' values. Last but not least, they can also be used in **guard expressions**. You will find the complete list of functions at `http://lesscss.org/functions/`.

In this chapter, you won't find all these functions, but you will learn how to use functions from all different groups. Functions can be grouped based on their input and output types; these types are mathematical functions, color functions, list functions, string functions, and type functions. There are also a small number of functions that can't be grouped using the preceding classification.

JavaScript

The Less functions map the native JavaScript functions and code in the first place, because of the fact that Less has been written in JavaScript. Currently, the JavaScript expressions can still be evaluated as values inside the Less code, but this ability may be removed in future versions. The JavaScript code should be wrapped between back quotes when used in your Less code, as shown in the following code:

```
@max:
  ~"`Math.max(10,100)+
    'px'`";
p {
  width: @max;
}
```

This Less code, which includes JavaScript code, will compile into the following CSS code:

```
p {
   width: 100px;
}
```

Even though it is possible, try to avoid using JavaScript in your code. The Less compilers written in other languages can't evaluate this code, so your code is not portable and is more difficult to maintain.

If there is no built-in Less function available for your purpose, try to write the equivalent code of what you need in Less code. Since Version 1.6, there is a max() function, but prior to that you could use the following code:

```
.max(@a,@b) when (@a>=@b){@max:@a;}
.max(@a,@b) when (@b>@a){@max:@b;}
```

In particular, watch out when using the JavaScript environment in your Less code. Also, values such as document.body.height make no sense in your compiled and stateless CSS.

List functions

The extract() and length() functions are the functions to get the values and the length of a CSV list. Together, these functions can be used to iterate as arrays over a CSV list.

Remember the loop used to set the background images in *Chapter 2, Using Variables and Mixins*? Here, you will use the same technique to add icons before the links in the sidebar navigation.

 This example uses icons from **Font Awesome**. Font Awesome is an iconic font that uses scalable vector icons, which can be manipulated by CSS. Icons can be scaled or colored easily with CSS. Also, loading the font requires only one HTTP request for all icons. Refer to http://fontawesome.io/ for more information.

To use Font Awesome, reference its source first, by adding the following line of code to the head section of your HTML document:

```
<link href="//netdna.bootstrapcdn.com/font-awesome/4.3.0/css/font-
   awesome.css" rel="stylesheet">
```

> Font Awesome and other iconic fonts can also be integrated and compiled into your project using Less. You will learn how to do this in *Chapter 4, Testing Your Code and Using Prebuilt Mixins Libraries.*

In your HTML document, you can now use the following line of code:

```
<i class="fa fa-camera-retro"></i> fa-camera-retro
```

Icons are added with the CSS :before pseudo class, so the preceding HTML code can also be styled without a class, by using the following Less code:

```
i:before {
  font-family:'FontAwesome';
  content:"\f083";
}
```

> A list of the Font Awesome icons and their CSS content values can be found at http://astronautweb.co/snippet/font-awesome/.

With this information about iconic fonts, you can construct a loop that adds icons to the list items of your navigation, as shown in the following code:

```
@icons: "\f007","\f004","\f108","\f112","\f072","\f17c";
.add-icons-to-list(@i) when (@i > 0) {
  .add-icons-to-list((@i - 1));
  @icon_: e(extract(@icons, @i));
  li:nth-child(@{i}):before {
    font-family:'FontAwesome';
    content: "@{icon_}\00a0";
  }
}
.add-icons-to-list(length(@icons));
```

In the @icon_: e(extract(@icons, @i)); line, e() is a string function, and this function is the equivalent of escaping using ~"". Also note that in the content: "@{icon_}\00a0"; statement, \00a0 only adds an extra space that separates the icon from the link.

The icons in the @icons CSV list are randomly chosen. The recursive calling of the add-icons-to-list() mixin starts with the .add-icons-to-list(length(@icons)); call, where length(@icons) returns the number of items in @icons.

The Less code of the loop that adds icons to the list items should be added into `less/navicons.less`. After adding the code, open `http://localhost/indexnavicons.html` to see the results, which should look like the following screenshot:

Iconized hyperlinks built with Less and Font Awesome

The icon list in the preceding screenshot serves only as a demonstration, where, in fact, the icons are not even related to the hyperlinks. The absence of this relationship makes it difficult to find a use case at all. However, with your creative mind, I bet you can find one. Remember that CSS is used only for presentation and cannot modify HTML, so you can't set the links themselves using Less. However, creating a relationship between the hyperlinks and icons that already exist is possible, as shown in the following code:

```
#content a[href*="linux"]:before {
  font-family:'FontAwesome';
  content: "\f17c\00a0";
}
```

Here, `a[href*="linux"]` is a selector for all anchors with the word `linux` in their `href` attribute. After adding the preceding code to `less/styles.less`, you can view the results at `http://localhost/index.html`.

Using the color functions

The Less color functions can be split into functions for color definition, blending, operations, and channel manipulation.

Colors are defined in color channels. An RGB color has three channels: red, green, and blue. CSS2 used this RGB definition to declare colors, and CSS3 adds new definitions for the color declaration. These new definitions, such as HSL and HSV, are nothing more than transformations of the RGB values. The CSS3 color setting methods should be more intuitive and user friendly. For instance, HSL defines colors in three channels, which are hue, saturation, and lightness in this case. Less supports different types of color definitions, and has built-in functions for channel manipulation of the different types of color definitions. Less also supports different types of color definitions. Since CSS3, you can declare color values as the hexadecimal, RGB, RGBA (RGB colors with an additional alpha channel that sets the opacity), HSL, and HSLA (HSL colors with an additional alpha channel that also sets the opacity) colors. Of course, you are allowed to use the predefined cross-browser color names.

The compiled color values of Less' color definitions are not always defined as a hexadecimal color in the CSS code. If possible, the output of a color definition matches the CSS values, as shown in the following code:

```
.selector {
  color1: rgb(32,143,60);
  color2: rgba(32,143,60,50%);
  color3: hsl(90, 100%, 50%);
  color4: darkblue;
}
```

The preceding Less code becomes the following CSS code after compilation:

```
.selector {

  color1: #208f3c;

  color2: rgba(32, 143, 60, 0.5);

  color3: #80ff00;

  color4: darkblue;

}
```

In the preceding code, `darkblue` is a color keyword name. The extended list of the color keyword names contains 147 color names. A complete list of the color keyword names can be found at http://meyerweb.com/eric/css/colors/.

Colors are a basic part of the design and styling of your website. The color functions can help you design your color palettes and make them dynamic. They will be used, for instance, to give elements a border color that is darker than the background color, or to give elements contrasting colors that are based on a single input color.

The darken() and lighten() functions

The darken() and lighten() functions are the two color functions that can be used to obtain a darker or lighter variant of the input color. You have seen how these functions have been used in the example layout from *Chapter 2*, *Using Variables and Mixins*. Now, you can apply these functions on the website navigation menu you built previously.

Open less/variablesnav.less in your text editor and define your menu variables that are dependent on the main @menucolor parameter as follows:

```
@menucolor:                      green;
@menu-background-color:          white;
@menu-font-color:                @menucolor;
@menu-border-color:              darken(@menucolor,10%);
@menu-hover-background-color:    darken(@menucolor,10%);
@menu-hover-font-color:          white;
@menu-active-background-color:   lighten(@menucolor,10%);
@menu-active-font-color:         white;
```

After doing this, check your changes by opening http://localhost/indexnav.html in your browser. Now, you can modify the look of your navigation by only changing the color defined by the @menucolor variable. You will also find that setting @menucolor to a light color, such as pink or yellow, makes your fonts unreadable, due to the contrast not being high enough between the background color and the font color. High contrast plays an important role in web design. Designs with high contrast help you meet accessibility standards. It not only helps visually disabled or color blind people, but also influences those with normal vision, as humans are naturally in favor of high contrast color designs. This favor plays a role in the first impression of your website.

Calculating the right amount of contrast is not always easy. Also, in this case, you don't want to have to change all your font colors after changing the basic color. The contrast() function of Less will help you choose a color that can easily be seen against a colored background. In accordance with WCAG 2.0 (http://www.w3.org/TR/2008/REC-WCAG20-20081211/#relativeluminancedef), this function compares the **luma** (perceptual brightness) value and not the lightness of the colors. The luma() function itself is also a built-in color function.

The `contrast()` function accepts four parameters, but only the first parameter is required. The first parameter defines the color to be compared against; this is the background color in this particular case. The second and third parameters define the dark and light color, which are black and white by default. The fourth and last parameter sets a threshold. This threshold has been set to 43 percent by default and defines the luma. Colors above the threshold are considered as light, and `contrast()` returns the dark color that is already defined in the second parameter for these light colors.

Now, reopen `less/variablesnav.less` and change the navigating font colors according to the following code:

```
@menucolor:                      green;
@menu-background-color:          white;
@menu-font-color:                contrast(@menucolor);
@menu-border-color:              darken(@menucolor,10%);
@menu-hover-background-color:    darken(@menucolor,10%);
@menu-hover-font-color:          contrast(@menu-hover-background-
                                 color);
@menu-active-background-color:   lighten(@menucolor,10%);
@menu-active-font-color:         contrast(@menu-active-background-
                                 color);
```

To see more effects, change the `@menucolor` variable to different colors such as `yellow`, `pink`, `darkgreen`, or `black`, and observe the changes by opening `http://localhost/indexnav.html`. Keep in mind that the lightest color is white and the darkest is black, so `darken(black,10%);` or `lighten(white,10%);` won't have any effect and will compile into `#000000;` and `#ffffff;` respectively.

Manipulating colors

As mentioned earlier, Less provides you with many functions to manipulate colors. This book is not about color theory, so it handles only some examples of color manipulation. You can find more information about color theory at `http://www.packtpub.com/article/introduction-color-theory-lighting-basics-blender`.

Functions for color operations

With the `darken()`, `lighten()`, and `contrast()` functions, you have become acquainted with some of the color operations. Other operations include `saturate()`, `desaturate()`, `fadein()`, `fadeout()`, `fade()`, `spin()`, `mix()`, and `grayscale()`.

The functions accept one or more color values, with the percentage as an input parameter, and return a color.

The following table will show you an overview of the functions for color operations:

Function name	Description	Parameters	Example	Outcome	Compiled output
darken()	Decreases the lightness of a color in the HSL color space by an absolute amount	color, amount 0 to 100%	darken (hsl(0, 50%, 50%), 10%);	hsl(0, 50%, 40%)	#993333
lighten()	Increases the lightness of a color in the HSL color space by an absolute amount	color, amount 0 to 100%	lighten (hsl(0, 50%, 50%), 10%);	hsl(0, 50%, 60%)	#cc6666
desaturate()	Decreases the saturation of a color in the HSL color space by an absolute amount	color, amount 0 to 100%	desaturate (hsl(0, 50%, 50%), 10%);	hsl(0, 40%, 50%)	#b34d4d
saturate()	Increases the saturation of a color in the HSL color space by an absolute amount	color, amount 0 to 100%	saturate (hsl(0, 50%, 50%), 10%);	hsl(0, 60%, 50%)	#cc3333
fadein()	Decreases the transparency (or increase the opacity) of a color, making it more opaque	color, amount 0 to 100%	fadein (hsla(0, 50%, 50%, 0.5), 10%)	hsla(0, 50%, 50%, 60%)	rgba(191, 64, 64, 0.6);

Function name	Description	Parameters	Example	Outcome	Compiled output
`fadeout()`	Increases the transparency (or decrease the opacity) of a color, making it less opaque	color, amount 0 to 100%	`fadeout (hsla(0, 50%, 50%, 0.5), 10%)`	`hsla(0, 50%, 50%, 40%)`	`rgba(191, 64, 64, 0.4);`
`fade()`	Set the absolute transparency of a color. Can be applied to colors even if they already have an opacity value or not	color, amount 0 to 100%	`fade(hsl(0, 50%, 50%), 10%);`	`hsla(0, 50%, 50%, 10%)`	`rgba(191, 64, 64, 0.1);`
`spin()`	Rotates the hue angle of a color in either direction	color, angle (number of degrees)	`fade(hsl(0, 50%, 50%), 30);`	`hsl(30, 50%, 50%)`	`#bf8040`
`mix()`	Mixes two colors together in variable proportion	color1, colors2, weight (optional, percentage default to 50%)	`mix(#ffff00, #00ff00, 50%);`	`#80ff00`	`#80ff00`
`grayscale()`	Removes all saturation from a color in the HSL color space	color	`greyscale (hsl(0, 50%, 50%));`	`hsl(0, 0, 50%)`	`#808080`
`contrast()`	Selects one of the two colors that provides the greatest contrast with another	color, dark (color), light(color), threshold 0-100%	`contrast (hsl(90, 50%, 50%), darkblue, lightblue, 30%);`	dark blue	darkblue

A complete description of these functions can also be found at `http://lesscss.org/functions/#color-operations`.

Note that the color ranges from white to black and does not wrap around. So, as mentioned earlier, you can't darken the color black so that it becomes white.

If color definitions contain percentages, the operations change them with the absolute percentage of the input parameter. So, darken(hsl(90, 80%, 50%), 20%) becomes #4d8a0f;, which equals hsl(90, 80%,30%) and *not* hsl(90, 80%,10%). Of course, you will see the same effect as you manipulate the second channel, which defines saturation. For instance, desaturate(hsl(45, 65%, 40%), 50%) compiles into #756e57;, which equals hsl(45, 15%, 40%).

The mix() function is the last example of the color operations. The other functions are left for you as exercises.

```
@color: mix(blue, yellow, 50%);
.class {
  color: @color;
}
```

This will become the following code:

```
.class {
  color: #808080;
}
```

This mixture can also be seen in the following screenshot :

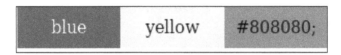

A mixture of blue and yellow presented using mix (blue, yellow, 50%)

Color blending with Less

The color blending functions calculate a new color based on two input colors, where functions apply basic operations such as subtraction on the color channels of the input colors. Available functions, also called blend modes, include multiply(), screen(), overlay(), softlight(), hardlight(), difference(), exclusion(), average(), and negation().

A complete overview of the color blending function can be found at `http://lesscss.org/functions/#color-blending`. The following table will give you a summary of the usage of these functions:

Function name	Description	Parameters	Example	Compiled output
`multiply()`	Multiplies two colors	color1, colors2	`multiply (#fffff00, #00ff00);`	`#00ff00`
`screen()`	Does the opposite of multiplication	color1, colors2	`screen (#fffff00, #00ff00);`	`#ffff00`
`overlay()`	Combines the effects of both `multiply()` and `screen()`	color1, colors2	`overlay (#fffff00, #00ff00);`	`#ffff00`
`softlight`	Similar to `overlay()` but avoids pure black	color1, colors2	`softlight (#fffff00, #00ff00);`	`#ffff00`
`hardlight`	The same as overlay but with the color roles reversed	color1, colors2	`hardlight (#fffff00, #00ff00);`	`#00ff00`
`difference()`	Subtracts the second color from the first color on a channel-by-channel basis	color1, colors2	`difference (#fffff00, #00ff00);`	`#ff0000`
`negation()`	Does the opposite of difference.	color1, colors2	`negation (#fffff00, #00ff00);`	`#ff0000`
`exclusion()`	A similar effect to difference with lower contrast	color1, colors2	`exclusion (#fffff00, #00ff00);`	`#ff0000`
`average`	Compute the average of two colors on a per-channel (RGB) basis	color1, colors2	`exclusion (#fffff00, #00ff00);`	`#80ff00`

Users of layered image editors such as Adobe Photoshop or GIMP will recognize these functions. **GIMP** is the **GNU Image Manipulation Program**. It is a freely distributed piece of software for such tasks as photo retouching, image composition, and image authoring. You can find GIMP at `http://www.gimp.org/`. The book, *Instant GIMP Starter, Fazreil Amreen, Packt Publishing*, will teach you the basics of GIMP through practical examples. You can find this book at `https://www.packtpub.com/hardware-and-creative/instant-gimp-starter-instant`.

The `difference()` function subtracts the second color from the first color on a channel-by-channel basis, as shown in the following code:

```
@color: difference(orange, red, 50%);
.class {
  color: @color;
}
```

The preceding code will become the following code:

```
.class {
  color:  #00a500;
}
```

The following screenshot shows how a mixture of orange and red would appear:

A mixture of orange and red appears using difference (orange, red, 50%)

Evaluating the type of an input value

The type functions evaluate the type of the input value and return as `true` if the type matches the function. The functions available are `isnumber()`, `isstring()`, `iscolor()`, `iskeyword()`, `isurl()`, `ispixel()`, `isem()`, `ispercentage()`, and `isunit()`. Some example functions are shown in the following code:

```
isnumber("string"); // false
isnumber(1234); // true
isnumber(56px); // true
iscolor(#ff0); // true
iscolor(blue); // true
iscolor("string"); // false
ispixel(1234); // false
ispixel(56px); // true
```

The type functions are useful in defining guards. Consider the following syntax:

```
.mixin(@value) when (isprecentage(@value)) {
  width: @value;
}
.mixin(@value) when (ispixel(@value)) {
  width: (@value / 4 );
}
```

The `default()` function is another built-in function that is not grouped in a function class. The `default()` function can be used inside a guard and returns as `true` when none of the other mixins match the caller. You can add a default mixin to the preceding mixins, as shown in the following code:

```
.mixin(@value) when (ispercentage(@value)) {
  width: 25%;
}
.mixin(@value) when (ispixel(@value)) {
  width: (@value / 4 );
}
.mixin(@value) when (default()) {
  display: none;
}
```

Extending Less with custom functions

When using Less in the browser, you can add not only plugins but also your own functions. Functions can be added with the `functions` option. You can use these functions in your Less code just like you used them with native functions.

Custom functions have lowercase names and return a value type defined by Less. Also, the input arguments should be types defined within Less.

In the following code, you will find an example of a custom function that returns twice its input:

```
var less = {
  functions: {
    twotimes : function(input) { return
      new(less.tree.Dimension)(input.value * 2);}
  }
}
```

Open `http://localhost/twotimes.html` in your browser and find the following Less code:

```
@width:50;
div {
  border: 1px solid black;
  width:unit(@width,px);
  &.big {
    width: unit(twotimes(@width),px);
  }
}
```

The preceding code compiles into CSS as follows:

```
div {
  width: 50px;
  border: 1px solid black;
}
div.big {
  width: 100px;
}
```

The `grunt-contrib-less` plugin for grunt, as described in *Chapter 1, Improving Web Development with Less*, also offers you the possibility of adding your own custom functions.

To add custom function to the command-line compiler, you should recompile your own version of Less, as described at `http://stackoverflow.com/questions/26607819/remove-properties-from-rendered-less-css/26610628`. Alternatively, you can write a plugin that provides your custom function. You can read how to write plugins with custom functions at `http://stackoverflow.com/questions/27809514/how-to-exend-the-less-compiler-with-a-custom-function-leveraging-a-plugin`.

The box-shadow mixin

With all that you have learned about Less, you can now understand, build, and evaluate any complex Less code. To prove this, open `less/mixins.less` and take a look at the `box-shadow` mixin (originally published at `http://lesscss.org/`), which looks like the following code:

```
.box-shadow(@style, @c) when (iscolor(@c)) {  box-shadow: @style
  @c;
}
```

```
.box-shadow(@style, @alpha: 50%) when (isnumber(@alpha)) {
  .box-shadow(@style, rgba(0, 0, 0, @alpha));
}
```

To fully understand these mixins, you will have to know the basics of `box-shadow` in CSS3. The `box-shadow` properties accept a CSV list of shadows. A shadow consists of a list of two to four length values and a color. The first two length values describe the vertical and horizontal offsets related to the center of the box. These values are required but can be set to `0` to get an equal-sized shadow around the box. The final values are optional and set the blur radius and the spread radius, respectively. The blur and spread radii are both `0` by default and give a sharp shadow, where the spread radius equals the blur radius.

Now, you should be able to evaluate the mixin. You will see that the mixins form a guard. Both mixins accept two parameters. The first parameter is the length vector, which was described earlier; the second is a color or a percentage. If you recall, the `isnumber(40%)` call evaluates as `true` despite the ending percent sign. Calling `rgba(0, 0, 0, @alpha)` will give shades of gray depending on the value of `@alpha`. If you define the second parameter as a color, such as `blue` or `#0000ff#`, the `iscolor(@c)` guard will evaluate as `true`, and the first mixin will be compiled using your defined color.

The original code published at `http://lesscss.org/` also contains some vendor prefixes for the `box-shadow` property. Using the Less `autoprefix` plugin or the `-prefix-free` library will be the best practice to add vendor prefixes.

Summary

In this chapter, you built a navigation menu with Less. The navigation contains, among other things, hovers, contrast colors, and icons that can all be set with a few basic settings. You have learned how to use the nesting rules, mixins, and built-in functions in Less. You were even introduced to writing your own functions. By the end of the chapter, you have understood and used the complex Less code. All this newly acquired knowledge will be very useful in the next chapter.

In the next chapter, you will learn how to find and build the reusable Less code. This will help you work faster and obtain better results.

4
Testing Your Code and Using Prebuilt Mixins Libraries

In the previous chapters, you learned how to use Less to compile your CSS code. Less helps you create a reusable and maintainable CSS code. You learned how to organize your files, and the preceding chapter also showed you the role of namespaces to make your code portable. Less helps you write efficient code to handle browser incompatibility. It doesn't solve problems with browser incompatibility on its own, but makes your solutions reusable, although the reusable mixins can still be complex for this reason. In this chapter, you will learn that you don't have to write all this complex code yourself. There are some libraries of prebuilt mixins out there that can help you work faster and create more stable code.

In this book, it's argued that using the autoprefixer to prefix your code will be best practice. As already mentioned, the autoprefixer adds neither nonstandard code nor polyfills to your CSS code. Polyfills are small pieces of code, mostly JavaScript, that provide technology for a browser that is not supported natively.

Some other plugins can add nonstandard code too. For instance, the Pleeease plugin for Less (`https://github.com/bassjobsen/less-plugin-pleeease`) can add the `filter` property for the Internet Explorer 8 browser to set the opacity.

Although, in most cases, the mixin libraries are not needed for single-line declaration any more, many other use cases can still be found.

This chapter will cover the following topics:

- Revisiting the CSS background gradients
- Preventing unused code
- Testing your code

- Using libraries with prebuilt mixins
- CSS3 animations
- Retina.js

Revisiting the CSS background gradients

Remember the CSS3 background gradient that was discussed in *Chapter 2, Using Variables and Mixins*? To show a better or the same gradient on different browsers, you have to use vendor-specific rules. Different sets of rules make your mixins more complex. In this case, more complex also means more difficult to maintain.

In practice, your mixins grow with outdated code or with code that is no longer supported on the one hand, while on the other hand, you have to update your mixins for newer browsers. Of course, we can only hope that new browser versions support the CSS3 specifications without any further changes to the code.

The Can I use... website (http://caniuse.com/) provides compatibility tables for the HTML5, CSS3, and SVG support, and also for desktop and mobile browsers. It will show you that most of the current browsers have support for the CSS gradients in their current versions. Currently, older versions of the Android browser for mobile still relies on the -webkit vendor rule, and Opera Mini doesn't support it at all.

If you drop the support for older browsers, your mixin can be reduced to the following code snippet:

```
.verticalgradient(@start-color: black; @end-color: white;
  @start-percent: 0%; @end-percent: 100%) {
  background-image: -webkit-linear-gradient(top, @start-color
    @start-percent, @end-color @end-percent);
  background-image: linear-gradient(to bottom, @start-color
    @start-percent, @end-color @end-percent);
  background-repeat: repeat-x;
}
```

The preceding code also drops support for IE8 and IE9. If you choose to support these browsers too, you have to add an additional IE-specific rule. The Can I use... website also shows you the market shares of the most common browsers.

 Note that you don't need a vendor prefix at all if you drop support for the Android browser below release 4.4 or decide to use auto-prefixing.

In some cases, it can also be useful to only provide functional support for older browsers and not expect everything to look exactly the same on all the browsers. For instance, a navigation structure without advanced animations can still help the user navigate through your site. People who use an older browser do not always expect the newest techniques. These techniques also do not always have added values. Older browsers mostly don't run on the newest hardware; on these browsers, support for features such as gradients will only slow down your website instead of adding any value. The preceding strategy will be called graceful degradation.

As you can see, creating background gradients with full browser support is not that easy. Depending on your situation, you can use different strategies to solve this problem. In *Chapter 1, Improving Web Development with Less*, you already read about how to prefix your code. Older browsers like Internet Explorer version 7 and 8 need polyfills or alternative syntaxes to support background gradients. Also, the calculation of the angle and keywords has changed over time. Most of these issues are already discussed in *Chapter 2, Using Variables and Mixins*. The prefix-free library offers solution for support for browsers including Internet Explorer release 9. You can read more about this in Verou's blog post at `http://lea.verou.me/2012/07/important-prefix-free-update/`. Also, the Less `autoprefix` plugin does not add polyfills to support older versions of Internet Explorer.

In *Chapter 6, Using the Bootstrap 3 Frontend Framework*, we will discuss Bootstrap 3. Bootstrap 3 is a HTML, CSS, and JS framework for developing responsive, mobile first projects on the web. Bootstrap's CSS code has been built with Less. You can reuse Bootstrap's Less code for background gradients to create the CSS code with full browser support.

You can download Bootstrap's source code, including all the Less code, from `http://getbootstrap.com/getting-started/`. Now, remember the directive gradients from *Chapter 2, Using Variables and Mixins*. Bootstrap's Less code contains mixins for different types of gradients. All gradient mixins have been wrapped in the `#gradient` namespace.

To reuse Bootstrap's gradient mixins, you can use the following code:

```
@import: "bootstrap-master/less/mixins/gradients.less";
.gradient {
  #gradient > .directional(red, blue, 90deg);
}
```

Open `http://localhost/bootstrapgradient.html` in your browser, and you will find that your gradient applied on the body looks like the following screenshot:

Background gradient generate with Bootstrap's gradient mixin

The preceding screenshot shows you that Bootstrap can also be used as a mixin library for non Bootstrap projects.

Unused code

Even when using Less for long running and growing projects, it's almost impossible to not find some unused pieces of code in your code. Browsers still try to apply this unused code, which may cause pretty significant performance hits, both in terms of network transfers as well as rendering time. Browser tools can help detect this unused code in your final CSS code.

Chrome's developer tools

Google Chrome's developer tools have an option to find the unused CSS code. In Google Chrome, navigate to **Tools | Developers Tools**, select the **Audits** tab, and click on **Run**.

Now, use this tool to test the demo code from the previous chapters.

To start, open `http://localhost/index.html` in your browser and run the test. You will see the following screenshot:

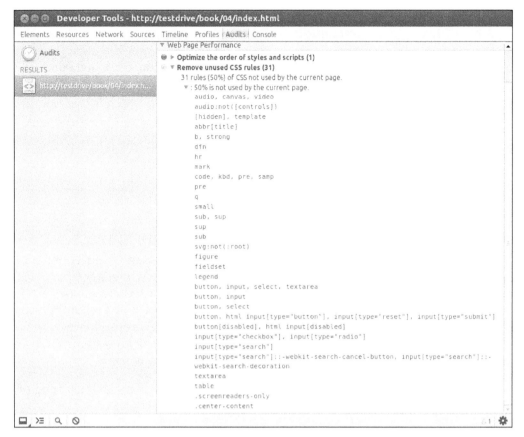

Unused code shown by Chrome's developer tools

The list of unused code starts with a long list of styles defined in `less/normalize.less`, as seen in *Chapter 1, Improving Web Development with Less*; these are the styles of the CSS reset.

In most projects, the same base of the CSS code (the same file) is used for every page. For this reason, you cannot always guarantee that a page includes only the code that it really uses. Some of this code won't be used on every page but will have to be used on other or future pages. Web browsers are able to cache the CSS files; for this reason, it is better to use the same CSS file to style different pages from your website. Some pages will not use all the cached style rules, which will be shown as unused code on that page. Cached code is loaded once and used on every page. The CSS reset seems useful for all pages, so you should not change or remove it.

As you can also see, `.centercontent` and `.screen-readeronly` are unused. Remember that classes are compiled into your CSS code while mixins are not, and `.centercontent` and `.screen-readeronly` are defined as classes. Having a `.screen-readeronly` class seems useful, but `.centercontent` can be changed to a mixin.

Firebug CSS usage add-on

For Firefox, an add-on for Firebug is available. This helps you find the unused code. You can download this plugin from `https://addons.mozilla.org/en-US/firefox/addon/css-usage/`.

Testing your code

You don't have to write all the Less code yourself as it is reusable and portable. Mixins and snippets of the Less code can be found on the Web and (re)used in your projects. Search for the Less mixin background gradients and you will get many useful hits. Try to find a code that offers support for browsers and meets your requirements. If you have any doubts about the browser support of a mixin, consider asking questions on **Stackoverflow.com** (`http://www.stackoverflow.com/`). Always show your code and what you have done; don't just ask for a solution. Also, other questions regarding Less can be asked on Stackoverflow.com too.

Integration of code snippets, or even complete namespaces. will make the testing of your code more important.

Understanding TDD

Test-driven development (TDD) is a proven method for software development. In TDD, you write tests for every piece of code in your project. All tests should pass after changing your code; whether when adding or improving functionalities, or when refactoring the code. All tests should run automatically. While automatically testing the Less and CSS code, you need to manually look at the exact appearance of the pages in different browsers and devices, although other aspects such as correctness and performance can be tested automatically. You can, for instance, automatically test your code with tools such as **CSS Lint** (`http://csslint.net`). CSS Lint validates and tests your code, among other things, for performance, maintainability, and accessibility. These tools test the compiled CSS code and not your Less code. The Less Lint Grunt plugin compiles your Less files, runs the generated CSS through CSS Lint, and outputs the offending Less line for any CSS Lint errors that are found. More information can be found at `https://www.npmjs.org/package/grunt-lesslint`.

All about style guides

A style guide gives an oversight of your website's elements, such as buttons, navigation structures, headings, and fonts. It shows the elements in the right presentation and colors. Creating style guides for your project and website can help you test your Less code. Style guides will also help other developers and content publishers of your project.

You may be thinking now that the style guides are indeed useful but are time consuming, for this reason, **StyleDocco** and the `tdcss.js` framework will be discussed in the next sections. These tools generate your style guides automatically based on your Less (or compiled CSS) code. Both tools still require some additional code and effort, but it won't take too much of your time. Testing your code nearly always pays you back. Also, realize the big win here: you only have to test the effect of your styles. Less guarantees that your CSS code is already valid, and the Less compiler handles its optimization. As promised, it provides more time for your real design tasks.

When your team gets different roles for coding and testing, you should prefer the `tdcss.js` framework, because this tool does not require changes in your Less code.

Building a style guide with StyleDocco

StyleDocco generates documentation and style guide documents from your style sheets. StyleDocco works very well with the Less files too. To create a style guide with StyleDocco, you will have to add comments to your Less files. The comments should explain what the style does, and also contain the HTML example code. The comments need to be written in **Markdown**. Markdown is a plain text format that can be easily converted into HTML. StackOverflow.com uses Markdown for posts and comments. You can use its help guide to learn more; you will find it at http://www.stackoverflow.com/editing-help/.

StyleDocco can be installed with npm using the following command:

```
npm install -g styledocco
```

You read about npm in *Chapter 1*, *Improving Web Development with Less*. After installing StyleDocco, you will have to add the Markdown comments to your Less files.

To see an example of a style guide generated with StyleDocco, open `less/nav.less` in your text editor and add the description in Markdown, followed by the HTML test code, as shown in the following code snippet:

```
/* Construct a navigation structure.

  <ul class="nav">
    <li><a href="#">item 1</a></li>
    <li><a href="#">item 2</a></li>
    <li class="active"><a href="#">item 3</a></li>
  </ul>
*/
```

To build your style guide, navigate to your Less folder (`less`) in the terminal and run the following command:

```
styledocco -n "Less Web Development Essentials Styleguide"
--preprocessor "/usr/local/bin/lessc"  --verbose
```

In the preceding example, the name of the style guide is set with `-n`. Mostly, you don't have to set the `-preprocessor` option if your file path contains the Less files only. To build a style guide for your Less files, the command, which does not require to navigate to your `less` folder first, will look as follows:

```
styledocco -n "Less Web Development Essentials Styleguide" less/*
```

The `styledocco` command generates a new folder named `docs/`. This folder contains an `index.html` file, which can be opened in your browser. The final result will look like the following screenshot:

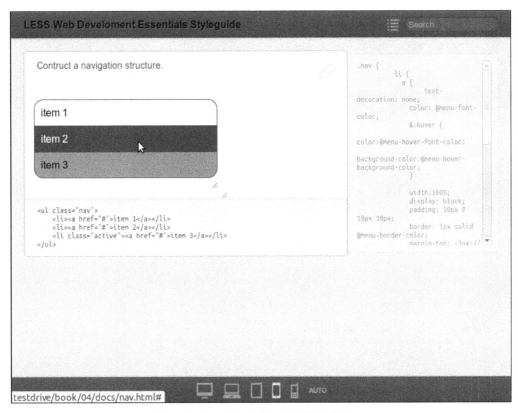

Example of a style guide built with StyleDocco

Testing your code with tdcss.js

The tdcss.js framework is another style guide tool that works well with Less, and promotes the usage of test-driven development. The tdcss.js framework can be downloaded free of charge from GitHub at https://github.com/jakobloekke/ tdcss.js. Also, see http://jakobloekke.github.io/tdcss.js/ for further information. Unlike StyleDocco, using tdcss.js doesn't change your Less files. You generate your style guide with snippets of relevant source code from your project. You can use the HTML-comment-style coding, for instance, <!-- : Navigation -->, to separate them. Snippets are copied and pasted to an HTML document, which forms your style guide, and includes styles from your Less code and tdcss.js. The head section of the HTML document of the example navigation will have the following structure:

```
<!-- Your Less code   -->
  <link rel="stylesheet/less" type="text/css"
    href="less/styles.less" />
```

```
    <script type="text/javascript">less = { env: 'development'
      };</script>
    <script src="less.js" type="text/javascript"></script>

  <!-- TDCSS -->
    <link rel="stylesheet" href="tdcss/tdcss.css" type="text/css"
      media="screen">
    <script
      src="http://code.jquery.com/jquery-1.11.0.min.js"></script>
    <script
      src="http://code.jquery.com/jquery-migrate-1.2.1.min.js">
        </script>

    <script type="text/javascript" src="tdcss/tdcss.js"></script>
    <script type="text/javascript">
      $(function(){
        $("#tdcss").tdcss();
      })
    </script>
```

The markup in the body is as follows:

```
<div id="tdcss">
  <!-- # Navigation -->
  <!-- & Style lists used for navigation. -->
  <!-- : Basic navigation -->
    <ul class="nav">
      <li><a href="#">item 1</a></li>
      <li><a href="#">item 2</a></li>
      <li class="active"><a href="#">item 3</a></li>
    </ul>
</div>
```

See the result of the preceding code by opening `http://localhost/tdcss.html` in your browser. The result will look like the following screenshot:

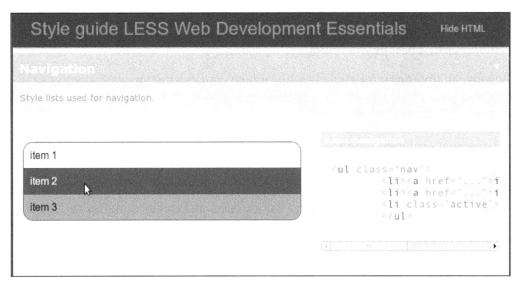

Example of a style guide built with tdcss.js

Prebuilt mixins

You already know about searching and finding mixins on the Web. However, using and reusing well-tested mixins will be a lot easier than that. Other developers have already built complete libraries of prebuilt mixins, which you can use for your projects. In the past, mixins' libraries could help you use single-line declarations for the CSS properties that require prefixing. Nowadays, you should use autoprefixing to add vendor prefixes. In the next section, you will be introduced to some useful mixin libraries. Following is a list of the libraries you will get acquainted with:

- **Less Elements** (http://lesselements.com)
- **Less Hat** (http://lesshat.madebysource.com/)
- **3L** (http://mateuszkocz.github.io/3l/)
- **Clearless** (http://clearleft.github.com/clearless/)
- **Preboot** (http://markdotto.com/bootstrap/)
- **More-or-less** (https://github.com/pixelass/more-or-less)
- **Less-bidi** (https://github.com/danielkatz/less-bidi)

A more comprehensive list of the mixin libraries can also be found at http://lesscss.org/usage/#frameworks-using-less.

Understand that you don't have to choose; there is no restriction that you have to use only one of these libraries. All these libraries have pros and cons; you have to choose the libraries that best fit your project requirements.

Globally, all libraries offer you a Less file which contains the mixins that you can import in your project. Although some libraries also have some settings, in all cases, `@import "{library-name}";` will be enough to make its mixins available for your project. Less has no restrictions on including more than one library, but doing this will give you problems with the clashing mixin names. All mixins with the same name will be compiled into the CSS code (if their parameters also match). For this reason, some libraries also have a prefixed version of these mixins.

Instead of the prefixed versions, using namespaces, as explained in *Chapter 3, Nested Rules, Operations, and Built-in Functions*, offers a more stable solution in most cases, as shown in the following code snippet:

```
// create a namespace for {library-name}
#{library-name}{@import "{library-name}";}
```

Make the mixins available using `#{library-name} > mixin()`.

The Less code for some libraries can also be preloaded by using a preprocess plugin, as described in *Chapter 3, Nested Rules, Operations, and Built-in Functions*. When a Less plugin for a library used is already available, it will be mentioned in the text too.

Creating gradients and layouts with Less Elements

Less Elements is perhaps the most compact library of the ones discussed in this chapter. Compact doesn't mean it is not useful.

Remember the vertical background gradient from the beginning of the chapter? You have seen that you will need at least three declarations, including vendor-specific rules, when you are supporting modern browsers.

With Less Elements, you can do the same with a single declaration of the Less code with three parameters, as shown in the following code snippet:

```
element {
  .gradient(#F5F5F5, #EEE, #FFF);
}
```

The first parameter defines the fallback color, used for browsers that don't support gradients. The gradient goes from bottom to top, where the second parameter sets the bottom color, and the third parameter sets the top color.

The preceding Less code will finally compile into CSS as follows:

```
element {
  background: #f5f5f5;
  background: -webkit-gradient(linear, left bottom, left top,
    color-stop(0, #eeeeee), color-stop(1, #ffffff));
  background: -ms-linear-gradient(bottom, #eeeeee, #ffffff);
  background: -moz-linear-gradient(center bottom, #eeeeee 0%,
    #ffffff 100%);
  background: -o-linear-gradient(#ffffff, #eeeeee);
  filter:
    progid:DXImageTransform.Microsoft.gradient
      (startColorstr='#ffffff', endColorstr='#eeeeee',
        GradientType=0);
}
```

In its simplicity, Less Elements offers many useful mixins to build your project with the CSS3 techniques. It provides single-line declarations for all CSS3 properties with vendor-specific rules, and extends this with declarations for layout. When you are using the Less `autoprefix` plugin, you do not need the single-line declarations in most cases any more. For full browser support, the background gradient mixins are still useful, as they provide the `filter` declarations for older versions of the Internet Explorer browsers and a fallback color, as explained before.

In the next section, you will find an example of a layout declaration provided by Less Elements. The `.columns()` mixin divides an element into columns, including a border and a gap between the columns. Variables for the `.columns()` mixin are in the order of column width, column count, column gap, column border color, column border style, and column border width.

This mixin can be applied on non-replaced block-level elements (except the table elements), table cells, and inline-block elements, such as the `body` or `div` elements.

To divide a `div` element in three columns with a width of 150 px, you can now write the following code in Less:

```
div.threecolumns {
  .columns(40px, 3, 20px, #EEE, solid, 1px);
}
```

The preceding code compiles into CSS and looks as shown in the following code snippet:

```
div.threecolumns {
    -moz-column-width: 150px;
    -moz-column-count: 3;
    -moz-column-gap: 20px;
    -moz-column-rule-color: #eeeeee;
    -moz-column-rule-style: solid;
    -moz-column-rule-width: 1px;
    -webkit-column-width: 150px;
    -webkit-column-count: 3;
    -webkit-column-gap: 20px;
    -webkit-column-rule-color: #eeeeee;
    -webkit-column-rule-style: solid;
    -webkit-column-rule-width: 1px;
    column-width: 150px;
    column-count: 3;
    column-gap: 20px;
    column-rule-color: #eeeeee;
    column-rule-style: solid;
    column-rule-width: 1px;
}
```

You can also test this by loading `http://localhost/columns.html` in your browser. Also, resize your browser window from small screen to full screen to see that these columns are responsive by default. The compiled `.div.threecolumns` class can be used with the following HTML code:

```
<div class="threecolumns" role="content">Vestibulum at dolor
aliquam, viverra ipsum et, faucibus nunc. Nulla hendrerit tellus
eu sapien molestie adipiscing. Cras ac tellus sed neque interdum
egestas sit amet vel diam. Aenean congue dolor et elit blandit
commodo. Pellentesque dapibus tellus eu augue ullamcorper dignissim.
Pellentesque pretium a dui a consequat. Curabitur eleifend lectus
vel viverra mollis. Sed egestas bibendum tortor mattis fermentum.
Suspendisse pellentesque facilisis blandit.</div>
```

The preceding code will result in the following screenshot:

Header

Vestibulum at dolor aliquam, viverra ipsum et, faucibus nunc. Nulla hendrerit tellus eu sapien molestie adipiscing. Cras ac tellus sed neque interdum egestas sit amet vel	diam. Aenean congue dolor et elit blandit commodo. Pellentesque dapibus tellus eu augue ullamcorper dignissim. Pellentesque pretium a dui a consequat.	Curabitur eleifend lectus vel viverra mollis. Sed egestas bibendum tortor mattis fermentum. Suspendisse pellentesque facilisis blandit.

Example of a multicolumn layout built with the columns mixin of Less Elements

The `.columns()` mixin makes use of **CSS Multi-column Layout Module**. More information about this module can be found at `http://www.w3.org/TR/css3-multicol/`. Unfortunately, the support for this module from most modern browsers is not good yet.

Less Elements does not provide any information about the browser support of the compiled CSS code. You must have realized this when using Less Elements in your project. As mentioned earlier, you can check browser support on the Can I use website. To find out which browsers support this CSS Multi-column Layout Module, you will have to visit `http://caniuse.com/multicolumn`. Always check the preceding module with the requirements of your project. Also, this example shows you why style guides can be very useful.

Using the comprehensive Less Hat library

Unlike Less Elements, Less Hat is a very comprehensive library of mixins. Currently, it contains 86 prebuilt mixins. Less Hat also has a strong relationship with CSS Hat. CSS Hat is a commercial licensed tool that converts Adobe Photoshop layers into CSS.

The Less Hat mixins offer the possibility of disabling some browser-specific prefixes, as shown in the following code:

```
@webkit: true;
@moz: true;
@opera: true;
@ms: true;
@w3c: true;
```

In the preceding code, `@w3c` refers to the rules that define the standard property names, described by the W3C specification. Of course, standard property names do not have a prefix. In case you use the Less `autoprefix` plugin to compile your code, you should set all browser-specific variables, except the `@w3c` variable, to `false`. Less Hat advertises itself as having mixins that create an unlimited number of shadows, gradients, and animations. The `box-shadow` mixin is an example of this. With Less Hat, the `box-shadow` mixin can be written as `.box-shadow(<offset-x> <offset-y> spread blur-radius color inset, ...)`.

To try the preceding `.box-shadow` mixin, you can write it in Less with Less Hat as follows:

```
div {
  .box-shadow(30px 30px 5px green inset,-30px -30px 5px blue
    inset);
}
```

The preceding code compiles into the following code snippet:

```
div {


  box-shadow: 30px 30px 5px #008000 inset, -30px -30px 5px #0000ff
    inset;
}
```

To inspect this, open `http://localhost/boxshadow.html` in your browser and you will see the result of the `.box-shadow` mixin, as shown in the following screenshot:

Example of the effect of the box-shadow mixin of Less Hat

Indeed, the `.box-shadow()` mixin of Less Elements doesn't accept multiple shadows, but the mixin of 3L, which is discussed in the next section, works with multiple shadows separated with commas.

The lesshat mixin for the less.js plugin

When you are compiling your Less code on the command line, you can also use the `lesshat` mixin for the `less.js` plugin. This plugin imports the `lesshat` mixins before your custom code, which enables you to use any `lesshat` mixin, without explicitly importing the library in your code. You can find the `lesshat` mixin for the `less.js` plugin at `https://github.com/bassjobsen/less-plugin-lesshat/`.

The Less plugins can also be used when you compile your code with Grunt or Gulp as described in *Chapter 1, Improving Web Development with Less.*

Using the 3L library of prebuilt mixins

Lots of Love for Less (3L) is another collection of prebuilt mixins. 3L provides mixins for CSS reset or normalization, as discussed earlier in *Chapter 1, Improving Web Development with Less.* You can call these mixins, without placing them inside the selector blocks, as follows:

```
.normalize();

/* OR */
.reset();

/* OR */
.h5bp();
```

In the preceding `.h5bp()` reset, your CSS is based on **HTML5 Boilerplate**. HTML5 Boilerplate is a professional frontend template for building fast, robust, and adaptable web applications or sites. You can find more information on Boilerplate at `http://html5boilerplate.com/`. 3L not only offers a mixin for HTML5 Boilerplate's reset, but also contains mixins for HTML5 Boilerplate's helper classes. These mixins contain the clearfix and mixins, which change the visibility of content, depending on the device type.

For instance, `.visuallyhidden()` can be used to hide the content for browsers but have this content available for screen readers.

SEO and HTML debugging

Search engine optimization (SEO) plays an important role in modern web design. Correct and valid HTML5 is the requirement for SEO. Also, setting proper titles, using the `meta` tags for keywords, descriptions, and the `alt` attributes for images will help your website rank higher. A `meta` tag that sets the description of your document in your HTML header may look like that shown in the following code:

```
<meta name="description" content="Example code for layout in
    LESS">
```

3L's `.seo-helper()` mixin will give you a quick insight into the missing elements and attributes of a web page.

To use this mixin, after importing 3L.you can write it in Less as follows:

```
html {
    .seo-helper();
}
```

After using the `.seo-helper()` mixin, your HTML page will contain warnings about missing titles or `meta` tags, and show a red border around images with the missing `alt` attribute, as shown in the following screenshot:

3L's helper class makes the missing alt attributes visible

Visit `http://localhost/indexseo.html` to get more insight on how this class works. After this, you can judge for yourself whether this class is useful or not. Independent of your judgment, the `.seo-helper()` mixin shows you how Less can also be applied for functions other than a website's styles.

Using the Clearless library of prebuilt mixins

Clearless also has a relationship with HTML5 Boilerplate. Just like 3L, it offers mixins for the HTML5 Boilerplate and helper classes. Besides this, it also makes use of **Modernizr**. Modernizr is a JavaScript library that detects HTML5 and CSS3 features in the user's browser. Modernizr adds additional classes to the `html` element of your HTML for detected features.

With Modernizr, your `html` element will look as shown in the following code snippet:

```
<html id="modernizrcom" class="js no-touch postmessage history
    multiplebgs boxshadow opacity cssanimations csscolumns
    cssgradients csstransforms csstransitions fontface
    localstorage sessionstorage svg inlinesvg no-blobbuilder
    blob bloburls download formdata
    wf-proximanova1proximanova2-n4-active
    wf-proximanova1proximanova2-i4-active
    wf-proximanova1proximanova2-n7-active
    wf-proximanova1proximanova2-i7-active
    wf-proximanovacondensed1proximanovacondensed2-n6
    -active wf-athelas1athelas2-n4-active
    wf-active" lang="en" dir="ltr">
```

This list of class names tells you whether a feature is available or not. The browser used to produce the preceding code offers support for `box-shadow`, `opacity`, and so on. With Modernizr, you will have conditional classes that can be used in your Less code. Also, Clearless makes use of these classes.

Clearless has mixins for icons and the CSS sprite images. The latest available version of Clearless only uses the Modernizer classes for the icon mixins. In the *Passing rulesets to mixins* section in *Chapter 3*, *Nested Rules, Operations, and Built-in Functions*, you can find other use cases and examples of creating the CSS code for Modernizr with Less. Also, note that the Clearless library has not been updated recently. The mixins still work with the latest version of Less, and demonstrate how to write reusable code with Less.

The CSS sprite images is a technique that dates back at least seven years. A website's images are added to a single image, the sprite. If the browser requests an image, the sprite will be loaded as the background image. **SpriteMe** (`http://spriteme.org/`) can help you create sprites for your projects. CSS is used to show the requested image containing a part of the sprite. Loading one big sprite, which can be cached, instead of several small images, will reduce the number of HTTP requests needed by the browser to show the page. The fewer the HTTP requests, the faster the page will load.

In this section, you can read about how to create image sprites easily with Less and the Clearless library. You should note that this example is not intended to decide for you whether to use sprite images or not for your projects.

The data URIs are most used alternatives for sprite images now. Less supports the data URIs too. The data URIs enable you to include the content of a resource in your CSS as a `base64` encoded string.

Consider the following Less code that uses a data URI to include an image:

```
div {
    background-image: data-uri('images/less-sprite.png');
}
```

The preceding Less code will output the following CSS code. Note that the `base64` value in this code had been shortened.

```
div {
    background-image:
        url("data:image/png;base64,iVBORw0KGgoAAAANSUhE..==");
}
```

When compiling your Less code in browser, `data-uri()` generates a `url()` syntax for the image. The data URI will also be replaced with the `url()` syntax for images larger than 32KB, when compiling your code without the `--no-ie-compat` option. Although the `data-URI` method does not even need an extra HTTP request for the sprite image, the data URIs do not always load faster. You can read more about the performance of images sprites versus data URIs at `http://www.mobify.com/blog/css-sprites-vs-data-uris-which-is-faster-on-mobile/`.

To demonstrate the sprite mixins of Clearless, use the simple sprite of the Less image from the code bundle of this chapter (`less-sprite.png`), as shown in the following screenshot:

Example of a simple sprite image

To use the sprite image, you can write it in Less as follows:

```
#clearless {
    @import "clearleft-master/mixins/all.less";
    @sprite-image: "../images/less-sprite.png";
    @sprite-grid: 80px; //image height
}
```

```
.logo {
  #clearless > .sprite-sized(0,0,200px,80px);
  &:hover {
    #clearless > .sprite-sized(0,1,200px,80px);
  }
}
```

This code is also available in `less/sprite.less`. Note that the `#clearless` namespace has got its own scope, so `@sprite-grid` and `@sprite-grid` should be defined inside the namespace. Variables are set by redeclaration.

The compiled CSS code of the preceding code will look as follows:

```
.logo {
  background-image: url("../images/less-sprite.png");
  background-repeat: no-repeat;
  background-position: 0px 0px;
  width: 200px;
  height: 80px;
}
.logo:hover {
  background-image: url("../images/less-sprite.png");
  background-repeat: no-repeat;
  background-position: 0px -80px;
  width: 200px;
  height: 80px;
}
```

Load `http://localhost/index.html` to see the effect of the preceding code.

Finally, it should be mentioned that Clearless defines some mixins to construct a grid. These mixins will be explained to you in the next section because they are adopted from Preboot.

Using Preboot's prebuilt mixins for your project

Preboot was originally written by Mark Otto (@mdo) and is a comprehensive and flexible collection of the Less utilities. Preboot is the predecessor of Twitter's Bootstrap. Bootstrap is a frontend framework for developing responsive, mobile-first projects on the Web. You will learn more about Bootstrap in *Chapter 6, Using the Bootstrap 3 Frontend Framework*. Bootstrap improved the original Preboot code. Many of the Less variable and mixin improvements from Bootstrap were brought back in Preboot 2.

Preboot comes with mixins to build a grid system because of its relationship with Bootstrap. This grid system creates a row that contains 12 columns. Open `http://localhost/prebootgrid.html` from the downloaded code bundle in your browser to see an example with two rows. The first grid row contains three columns and the second row contains two columns. This grid is responsive by default; you can see this by making your browser window smaller, using the example grid. If the screen width is less than 768 pixels, the columns in the grid will stack under each other instead of being horizontal. The following code example shows only the compiled CSS code, without the responsive classes.

With Preboot, you can write the following code in Less:

```
.col-a-half {
  .make-column(6);
}
```

The preceding code compiles into CSS as follows (it is nonresponsive):

```
.col-a-half {
  min-height: 1px;
  padding-left: 15px;
  padding-right: 15px;
  -webkit-box-sizing: border-box;
  -moz-box-sizing: border-box;
  box-sizing: border-box;
  float: left;
  width: 50%;
}
```

In *Chapter 5*, *Integrating Less in Your Own Projects*, you will find another example that makes use of the Preboot's grid and discusses its responsive nature in more detail.

Preboot sets some variables to define the grid, as shown in the following code snippet:

```
// Grid
// Used with the grid mixins below
@grid-columns:          12;
@grid-column-padding:   15px; // Left and right inner padding
@grid-float-breakpoint: 768px;
```

Also, other values such as basic colors are predefined, as follows:

```
// Brand colors
@brand-primary:            #428bca;
@brand-success:            #5cb85c;
@brand-warning:            #f0ad4e;
@brand-danger:             #d9534f;
@brand-info:               #5bc0de;
```

In fact, Preboot is not a complete CSS framework, however, it's more than just a library of prebuilt mixins.

Using the more-or-less library

In contrast, Less has the `more-or-less` library that does not make use of inline JavaScript for mixins. In case you are using the Less `autoprefix` plugin, you do not need the single-line declarations. The `more-or-less` library also extends Less with some helpful functions such as the if-else-then declarations and the for loops. See the section about creating recursive loops in *Chapter 2, Using Variables and Mixins*, for more information about for loops.

The following Less code will show you how an if-else-then declaration will look:

```
@import 'less/more-or-less-master/less/fn/_if';

.color(@color) {
  .if(iscolor(@color), {
    .-then() {
      color: white;
    }
    .-else() {
      color: black;
    }
  });
}

div {
  &.white {
    .color(white);
  }
  &.none {
    .color(none);
  }
}
```

The preceding Less code will compile into the CSS code as follows:

```
div.white {
  color: white;
}
div.none {
  color: black;
}
```

The more-or-less library also offers you a for loop mixin, which enables you to rewrite the preceding mixin calls as follows:

```
div {
  @array: white, none;
  .for(@array); .-each(@value) {
    &.@{value} {
      .color(@value);
    }
  }
}
```

Although the preceding Less code possible looks more intuitive, you should realize that you can do the same by using guards, as described in *Chapter 2, Using Variables and Mixins*. Also, the for loops can be done with guards and the Less list functions. Inspect the following Less code to find out how to rewrite the preceding examples using guards:

```
.color(@color) {
  &.@{color} {

    & when (iscolor(@color)) {
      color: white;
    }

    & when not (iscolor(@color)) {
      color: black;
    }
  }
}

.loop(@colors; @i:1) when (@i <= length(@colors)) {

  @value: extract(@colors,@i);
  .color(@value);
  .loop(@colors; (@i + 1));
```

```
}

@array: white, none;

div {
   .loop(@array);
}
```

Less uses guards to keep syntax as close as possible to the declarative nature of CSS. Guards expressions and logic statements are similar to `@media` implementation in CSS. The `more-or-less` mixins are limited when building more complex logical statements while the native Less code is not. Those who are not familiar with using guards yet, can profit from the more intuitive syntax that the `more-or-less` library offers.

The Less-bidi library

When creating websites for Arabic, Hebrew, and other right-to-left scripts, you should change some CSS properties. For instance, `text-align: left` should become `text-align: right`. Less-bidi is a set of Less mixins that enables creating bi-directional styling, without significant code duplication. You can find this library at `https://github.com/danielkatz/less-bidi`.

How does it work? Instead of writing the `text-align` property directly in your code, you will use a mixin as follows:

```
.bidi-text-align(start);
```

Depending on the value of the `@bidi` variable, which can be left-to-right (`ltr`) or right-to-left (`rtl`), the output of the preceding mixin will change.

When you set `@bidi` to `ltr`, the output will be as follows:

```
text-align: left;
```

The same code with `@bidi` set to `rtl` will output the following CSS code:

```
text-align: right;
```

When compiling your Less code on the command line, you can use the `--modify-var` option of the `lessc` compiler to compile different versions of your CSS code with the same code base.

Use the following command to compile your CSS code for the right-to-left scripts:

```
lessc file.less --modify-var="bidi=rtl"
```

Instead of the Less-bidi library, you can also use the Less `css-flip` plugin. The Less `css-flip` plugin can be found at https://github.com/bassjobsen/less-plugin-css-flip. It generates the left-to-right (`ltr`) or right-to-left (`rtl`) CSS code from Less. This plugin post processes your compiled CSS code, so the advantage will be that you do not have to rewrite or change your Less code.

Finally, you should note that the W3C working draft for the `text-align` property already has the possibility to set the value to `start` or `end`. The `start` keyword will act as left if the text direction has been set to `ltr`, and `right` if direction is `rtl`. CSS Text Module Level 3 can be found at http://dev.w3.org/csswg/css-text-3/#text-align.

Integrating other techniques into your projects using Less

As well as prebuilt mixins, there are some other techniques that can be easily integrated in your projects using Less.

Creating animations with Less

When you think of CSS3, you automatically think of animations too. As already discussed in *Chapter 1, Improving Web Development with Less*, the CSS3 animations make CSS more powerful. HTML5 and CSS can easily replace Flash and other types of animations in many situations.

`Animate.css` is a library of cross-browser animations to use in your projects. You can find `Animate.css` at https://github.com/daneden/animate.css. `Animate.css` can easily be used with Less. On GitHub, you will also find some attempts to port the complete library to Less. In this example, you will only use a single animation from the library. The time functions of the CSS animations are described by `cubic-bezier` curves, so you can also create your own animation time functions at http://cubic-bezier.com/.

Animate.css comes with a `flipInX` effect. The CSS code of this effect will look as follows:

```
@keyframes flipInX {
  0% {
    transform: perspective(400px) rotate3d(1, 0, 0, 90deg);
    transition-timing-function: ease-in;
    opacity: 0;
  }
  40% {
    transform: perspective(400px) rotate3d(1, 0, 0, -20deg);
    transition-timing-function: ease-in;
  }
  60% {
    transform: perspective(400px) rotate3d(1, 0, 0, 10deg);
    opacity: 1;
  }
  80% {
    transform: perspective(400px) rotate3d(1, 0, 0, -5deg);
  }
  100% {
    transform: perspective(400px);
  }
}
```

You can save the preceding code in a file called `flipinx.less`. You will find a copy of this file, and the other files used in the example, in the code bundle of this book. After creating `keyframes`, as shown in the preceding code, you should also define the duration, delay, and number of iterations. Now, your Less code will look as follows:

```
h1 {
  backface-visibility: visible !important;
  animation-name: flipInX;
  animation-duration: 3s;
  animation-delay: 2s;
  animation-iteration-count: infinite;
}
```

For animations, you should use the Less `autoprefix` plugin or the `-prefix-free` library. If you cannot use these methods, you can also use the `more-or-less` library, as described in the *Using the more-or-less library* section. The `more-or-less` library contains mixins to set and prefix the duration, delay, and number of iterations of your animation too.

Open `http://localhost/flipinx.html` to see how the `flipInX` animation looks in your browser.

Using iconic fonts

As the name suggests, iconic fonts are sets of icons defined as a font. Iconic fonts can replace image icons in your projects. The main reason for using iconic fonts instead of images, and the reason they are discussed here is that iconic fonts, just like any normal font, can be fully manipulated with CSS. In your project, you can set the size, color, and shadows of the used iconic fonts with Less. The primary reason for using iconic fonts is to benefit the load time of your website; similar to the sprite images, only one HTTP request is needed to load them all. Iconic fonts will look good on different resolutions and displays too.

Iconic fonts were already used in *Chapter 3*, *Nested Rules, Operations, and Built-in Functions*. Font Awesome was loaded from CDN in the examples. Font Awesome also provides a bundle of the Less files from GitHub at `https://github.com/FortAwesome/Font-Awesome/tree/master/less`. You can use these files to integrate Font Awesome in your project by performing the following steps:

1. Copy the `font-awesome/` directory into your project.

2. Open your project's `font-awesome/less/variables.less` file and edit the `@fa-font-path` variable to point to your font directory, `@fa-font-path: "../font";`.

3. Import the Font Awesome Less file in your main Less file, `@import "font-awesome-4.0.3/less/font-awesome.less";`.

After performing the preceding steps, you can use the following snippet of code in your HTML document:

```
<ul class="fa-ul">
  <li><i class="fa-li fa fa-check-square"></i>List icons (like
    these)</li>
  <li><i class="fa-li fa fa-check-square"></i>can be used</li>
  <li><i class="fa-li fa fa-spinner fa-spin"></i>to replace</li>
  <li><i class="fa-li fa fa-square"></i>default bullets in
    lists</li>
</ul>
```

The preceding code, when opened in your web browser, will result in the following screenshot:

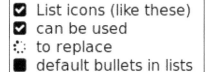

The HTML list with the Font Awesome items

You will find the Less code of the preceding HTML list in `less/font-awesome.less` of the downloadable files. Inspect this file. You will see that you don't have to change Font Awesome's original files to set `@fa-font-path`. The `@fa-font-path` variable will be set by redeclaration and will use the last declaration wins rule, as explained in *Chapter 2, Using Variables and Mixins*.

You can find more examples of the Font Awesome usage at `http://fontawesome.io/examples/`.

Also, other iconic fonts such as **Glyphicons** for Bootstrap can be used with Less (see `https://github.com/twbs/bootstrap/blob/master/less/glyphicons.less`). However, if you find iconic fonts without the Less files, you now have enough knowledge to create the required Less code yourself.

Try to write the required Less code to integrate **Meteocons** (`http://www.alessioatzeni.com/meteocons/`) into your project as an exercise, or perform the following steps:

1. Start by downloading the fonts from `http://www.alessioatzeni.com/meteocons/res/download/meteocons-font.zip`.

2. In this `zip` file, you will find four files: `meteocons-webfont.eot`, `meteocons-webfont.svg`, `meteocons-webfont.ttf`, and `meteocons-webfont.woff`. These are the different formats required to show the Meteocons in different browsers.

3. Copy these files to the `fonts/` folder of your project. You will also find `stylesheet.css` included with these font files. This file contains the `@fontface` styles for Meteocons. If you inspect the Font Awesome Less files, you will find the same kind of styles. The `@fontface` declaration is required to use the font in your project.

Now, you should remember the Less Hat prebuilt mixins. Less Hat has the `fontface` **mixin,** `.font-face(@fontname, @fontfile, @fontweight:normal, @fontstyle:normal)`.

Using this `fontface` mixin, you can add the following code to your Less code:

```
#lesshat {@import "lesshat/lesshat.less";}

@font-face {
  #lesshat > .font-face("Meteocons", "../fonts/meteocons-
    webfont");
}

[data-icon]:before {
  font-family: 'Meteocons';
  content: attr(data-icon);
}
```

The preceding code will compile into CSS as follows:

```
@font-face {
  font-family: "Meteocons";
  src: url("../fonts/meteocons-webfont.eot");
  src: url("../fonts/meteocons-webfont.eot?#iefix")
    format("embedded-opentype"),
      url("../fonts/meteocons-webfont.woff") format("woff"),
        url("../fonts/meteocons-webfont.ttf") format("truetype"),
          url("../fonts/meteocons-webfont.svg#Meteocons")
            format("svg");
  font-weight: normal;
  font-style: normal;
}
[data-icon]:before {
  font-family: 'Meteocons';
  content: attr(data-icon);
}
```

The preceding CSS code enables you to use the following HTML code:

```
<a href="" data-icon="A">Link</a>
```

The preceding code in HTML will look like the following screenshot:

Hyperlink with Meteocon

Earlier, you saw how the Font Awesome icons can be added by class name. To add this functionality to the Meteocons, you will have to write some Less code. The following diagram shows the letter for each icon of this font:

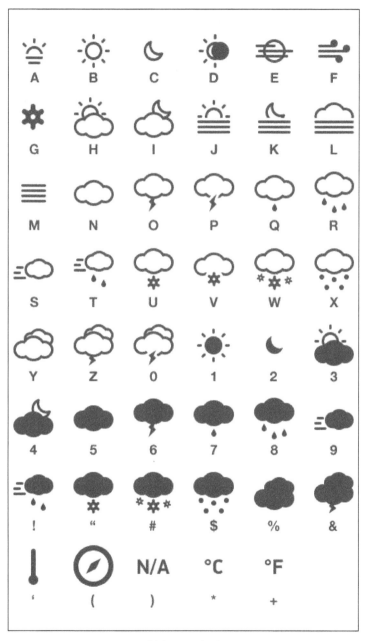

Meteocons font

Now, add a class declaration into your Less code for each icon as follows:

```
.  meteocons-sun                    { &:before { content: "\2a"; } }
```

In the preceding example, `.meteocons-sun` is your class name, and `\2a` represents the hexadecimal value of a similar character. 2A hexadecimal is 42 decimal, and the * (asterisk) has an ASCII value of 42. Instead of a hexadecimal value, you can also use octal or decimal (for the first 128 printable characters). Sometimes, `\u` of Unicode is prepended, such as `\u002a` in the preceding code.

If you do add these class declarations, your list will look like the following code snippet:

```
.mc-light-sunrise:before {
  content: "\0041";
}
.mc-light-sunshine:before {
  content: "\0042";
}
.mc-light-moon:before {
  content: "\0043";
}
.mc-light-eclipse:before {
  content: "\0044";
}
/*and so on*/
```

Now, you have the basics for an iconic font, and you can extend your code. For instance, add the following code to set the size of the font:

```
.mc-2x { font-size: 2em; }
.mc-3x { font-size: 3em; }
.mc-4x { font-size: 4em; }
.mc-5x { font-size: 5em; }
```

In the download section of this chapter, you will find the complete Less code to use Meteocons the same way as Font Awesome in `less/meteocons`. As you see, most of the Font Awesome's code can be reused. Visit `http://localhost/indexmeteo.html` to find out how to use this code.

Retina.js

High-density devices have more pixels per inch or centimeter than normal displays. Apple introduced the term **Retina** for its double-density displays. If you zoom in on an image (or scale it up), it will become blurred. This is the problem web designers have to solve when designing for high-density devices. You may be wondering what this has to do with Less. CSS, in combination with media queries (you will learn more about media queries in *Chapter 5, Integrating Less in Your Own Projects*), can prevent your images from becoming blurred on high-density displays.

To understand what happens, you have to realize that the CSS pixels are, in fact, device independent. The CSS pixels are used to give physical dimensions to the elements in the browser. On normal screens, a CSS pixel matches a device pixel. High-density displays have more device pixels than a CSS pixel; in the case of Retina, they have four times the number of pixels. More and smaller pixels make it impossible to see the individual pixels with the human eye and should thus give a better user experience.

Retina displays an image of 300 CSS pixels width that requires 600 device pixels in order to keep the same physical size. Now, you can prevent your images from blurring by using a bitmap with a higher resolution (the CSS pixels) and scale it down with HTML or CSS.

On a normal display, your HTML code will look as follows:

```
<img src="photo300x300.png" width="300px" height="300px">
```

While on a Retina display, you will show the same image with the following code snippet:

```
<img src="photo600x600.png" width="300px" height="300px">
```

Currently, there is a convention of adding @2x to the names of high-density images, such as example@2x.png.

You should now understand that you can use Less to write efficient code to give these different images the right CSS dimensions. The retina.js library (https://github.com/imulus/retinajs) helps you handle high-density images and displays; it combines JavaScript and Less to write your Retina code.

For normal images, you have to use the following code snippet:

```
<img src="/images/my_image.png"
  data-at2x="http://example.com/my_image@2x.png" />
```

The `data-at2x` attribute is only necessary if you want to specify a custom @2x image. If you just want to append @2x to the path, you can leave this off and it will be done automatically.

The preceding code will be handled by JavaScript, but you will have to use Less to set your background images. Here, background refers not only to the page background, but to every background set by CSS. Most modern designs use background images for layout; also, accessibility rules require decorative images set by CSS.

With `retina.js`, you can write the following code in Less:

```
.logo {
  .at2x('/images/my_image.png', 200px, 100px);
}
```

The preceding code will compile into CSS as follows:

```
.logo {
  background-image: url('/images/my_image.png');
}

@media all and (-webkit-min-device-pixel-ratio: 1.5) {
  .logo {
    background-image: url('/images/my_image@2x.png');
    background-size: 200px 100px;
  }
}
```

Also, the other libraries of prebuilt mixins mentioned earlier will have mixins to set the Retina backgrounds.

Summary

In this chapter, you learned how to keep your code clean and test it using style guides. You learned how to use libraries with prebuilt mixins, which help you develop your Less code faster and more securely. Last but not least, you also learned how to use Less and iconic fonts, and make your projects Retina-ready.

In the next chapter, you will learn how to integrate Less in your projects, or start a project from scratch with Less. You will also learn how to organize your project files and reuse your old CSS code. And finally, you will build a responsive grid with media queries.

5
Integrating Less in Your Own Projects

Now, it's time to integrate Less in your workflow and projects. In this chapter, you will learn how to migrate your current projects to using Less instead of plain CSS or start a new project from scratch using Less. We will discuss the techniques and tools to convert your CSS code into the Less code, and finally, you will learn how to build and use responsive grids using Less.

In this chapter, we will cover the following topics:

- Importing CSS into Less
- Migrating your projects to Less
- Starting a project from scratch
- Media queries and responsive design
- Using grids in your projects and designs

While working with Less and seeing how it addresses the problems of duplicate code and the inability to reuse your CSS, you would have wondered when you would be able to start using Less for your projects. Although this may be the most important question of this book, the answer is quite simple. You will have to start now! If you don't start now, you probably never will, and you will later end up spending too much time debugging your CSS code instead of working on your real design tasks. The CSS code is not DRY and reusable; this problem can be considered as the defect in your design process. There will never be an excuse to not solve the defects as soon as they are detected.

Importing CSS into Less

As you already know now, a valid CSS code is also a valid Less code. The CSS code can be imported into Less. There are different ways to do this. After importing your CSS, you can run the result through the compiler. This offers you an easy way to start using Less in your current project.

Consider creating a style guide before you start to import your CSS code. Style guides help you to test your code, as described in *Chapter 4, Testing Your Code and Using Prebuilt Mixins Libraries*. In addition, you must remember that Less is a CSS preprocessor. This means that you have to compile your Less code into CSS before taking it into production. Client-side compiling with `less.js` should only be used for test purposes! This is because client-side compiling may result in performance degradation and compiling the style sheets will take time. You will have to repeat the compiling process for every page request.

Only importing your CSS code, and then compiling it back into CSS again makes no sense. After importing, you should start improving your code. Importing CSS also gives you the opportunity to combine the preexisting CSS with the newly written Less code and allows you to do the conversion to Less iteratively and gradually.

Using the @import rule

Earlier, you saw that the `@import` rule in Less was used to import the Less files into your project. This rule in Less is an extended version of the same rule in CSS.

In the examples in the preceding chapters, the `@import` rule was only used to import the Less files. By default, each file is imported once. The complete syntax is as follows:

```
@import (keyword) "filename";
```

There are seven keywords that can be used with this rule: `reference`, `inline`, `less`, `css`, `once`, `multiple`, and `optional`. The `reference` keyword, for example, in `@import (reference) "file.less"` will make mixins and classes from `file.less` available without compiling them into the resulting CSS code.

This can be easily shown with an example. You can download all the example codes of all the chapters of this book from the Packt website (`www.packtpub.com`). The example layout from the preceding chapters will be used here again. Remember that the main file of this project, `styles.less`, imports the other project files. Now, you can use this to reuse the `navbar` component. Start the example by creating a new file and write the following code into it:

```
@import (reference) "styles";
.nav:extend(.nav all){};
```

These two lines will compile into the following code:

```
.nav {
  list-style: none outside none;
  padding: 0;
}
.nav li a {
  text-decoration: none;
  color: #000000;
  width: 100%;
  display: block;
  padding: 10px 0 10px 10px;
  border: 1px solid #004d00;
  margin-top: -1px;
}
.nav li a:hover {
  color: #ffffff;
  background-color: #004d00;
}
.nav li.active a {
  color: #000000;
  background-color: #00b300;
}
.nav li:first-child a {
  border-radius: 15px 15px 0 0;
}
.nav li:last-child a {
  border-radius: 0 0 15px 15px;
}
```

Note that the preceding result contains the values as defined in `variables.less` from the original project.

The `inline` keyword is used to import the code that is not compatible with Less. Although Less accepts standard CSS, comments and hacks won't get compiled sometimes. Use the `inline` keyword to import the CSS code as it is present in the output. As shown in the following code, the `inline` keyword differs quite a bit from the `css` keyword. The `less` keyword forces the imported code to be compiled. When using `@import (less)` `"styles.css"`, all the code will be compiled as usual. In the meantime, the `css` keyword forces `@import` to act as a normal CSS import. The following code shows the difference between `inline` and `css`:

```
@import (css) "styles.css";
```

The output of the preceding code is as follows:

```
@import "styles.css";
```

Imported style sheets (with `@import`) in your compiled CSS code are declared before all the other rules. These style sheets can play a role in the CSS precedence, which is discussed in *Chapter 1, Improving Web Development with Less*. For this reason, you cannot apply advanced techniques such as namespacing, and you should import files that are not created using Less at the beginning.

The CSS 2.1 user agents must ignore any `@import` rule that is present inside a block or after any non-ignored statement, other than `@charset` or `@import` (http://www.w3.org/TR/CSS21/syndata.html#at-rules). If you import a file with the same name twice, only one will be compiled by default. The same will happen if you use the `once` keyword. On the other hand, if you use the `multiple` keyword, the file will be compiled in the output twice. The following code shows an example of multiple output when you use the `multiple` keyword:

Consider a situation where the `styles.less` file contains the following code:

```
p {
  color: red;
}
```

Also, consider your Less code is as follows:

```
@import (multiple) "style";
@import (multiple) "style";
```

Then, the preceding code will output the following CSS code:

```
p {
  color: red;
}
p {
  color: red;
}
```

When you try to import a file that does not exist, the compiler will throw an error and stops compiling. The `optional` keyword can be used to import a file only when it exists. If you use the same code base for different projects, optional files can be useful to add or override some styles just by adding a file.

Migrating your project to Less

With the different import rules, you can start using Less in your project without having to change your code. After importing your CSS code, you can start defining variables and using mixins step by step. Always check the output of your new code before you start using it for production.

 Remember that style guides can help you to manage the migration of your project, and you have to compile your Less code on the server side into the CSS code before you can use it in production.

Organizing your files

Try to organize your files in the same way as the preceding examples. Create separate files for your project's variables and mixins. If your project defined a style sheet in `project.css` earlier, your main Less file may look, for instance, like the following code:

```
@import "reset.less";
@import "variables.less";
@import "mixins.less";
@import (less) "project.css";
```

The content for the `project.less` file has been discussed already in the *Preventing cross-browser issues with CSS resets* section in *Chapter 1, Improving Web Development with Less*. You will import your original `project.css` file in the preceding code; alternatively, you can rename it as `project.less`. In addition, note that you will finally compile a new CSS file, which will be used in your project. It's possible to use the same name for this file, but make sure that you do not overwrite your original CSS file if you want to keep it for reference. Although your new CSS files should apply the same styles, these files are better organized and Less guarantees that they contain only valid CSS. In addition, the compiler will compress the CSS file when you have the `--compress` option.

Converting the CSS code to the Less code

In the process of migration, you may not prefer to convert your code step by step. However, there are some available tools that can convert the CSS code to the Less code. These tools should be used with care. **Lessify** helps you organize your CSS code into the Less code. This tool puts rules for the same element or class together. You can use Lessify by visiting `http://leafo.net/lessphp/lessify/`.

Consider the following CSS code:

```css
p {
  color: blue;
}
p a {
  font-size:2em;
}
p a:hover {
  text-decoration: none;
}
```

After using Lessify, the preceding CSS code compiles into the following Less code:

```less
p {
  color:blue;
  a {
    font-size:2em;
  }
  a:hover {
    text-decoration:none;
  }
}
```

You can find another tool called **CSS2Less** at http://css2less.cc/. This tool also only groups the class and element rules. Lessify and CSS2Less can help you a little when you organize your styles. However, neither of the tools work with the media queries.

From all that you have learned so far, it seems like a good practice to start your project by developing your Less code. So, start your project by building a style guide using Less.

Your `project.less` file should look like the following code:

```
@import "reset.less";
@import "variables.less";
@import "mixins.less";
```

Integrate the `project.less` file with the client-side `less.js` compiler in your style guide. After this, start adding your design elements, or alternatively, you can add comments within your code.

When you are done with your style guide, you can start building your final HTML code. If you have to build a responsive website, you should first determine the screen sizes that you will need. For instance, mobile, tablet, and desktop can be a good choice.

To better understand how you can use Less at this stage of your process, the next two sections describe the role of CSS Media Queries in responsive design and teach you how to use grids.

Media queries and responsive design

Media queries is a CSS3 module and a W3C candidate recommendation since June 2012. The media queries module add the possibility to apply a style sheet to CSS only when a media query is evaluated as `true`. So, a media query has a condition that will be evaluated by the browser; you can compare this evaluation with an if…then statement.

A media query evaluates device's types and its features. Device's types are screen, speech, and print, among others, and its features are width, device-width, and resolution, among others.

Nowadays, the screen type and device's width play an important role in responsive web design. With the use of media queries, someone can restrict the CSS rules to a specified screen width, and thus, change the representation of a website with varying screen resolutions.

A typical media query will look like the following line of code:

```
@media  condition { ... }
```

For instance, the following media query sets the font color to black when viewport's width is larger than 767 pixels:

```
@media screen and (min-width: 768px) {
  color:black;
  //add other style rules here
}
```

In the preceding code, we can see that all the style rules between the accolades are only applied if the screen width is 768 pixels or larger. These style rules will follow the normal cascading rules.

Elastic measurement units in media queries

In the preceding example, the `min-width` property inside the media query was set by using pixels (`px`). Elastic measurement units (`em`) are an alternative for pixels and they seem to be more future proof. The `em` units are based on the font size and are relative to their parent. The `em` unit-based layouts react on the content when the users zoom or change the default font size.

Using the `em` units in media queries has one disadvantage; the `em` value in the media query will be based on the default font size of the browser or the default font size set by the user. This means that you do not have full control over the exact value of your break points. Using root elastic elements (`rem`) will solve this problem. The `rem` units are based on or are relative to the font size set for the `html` element (`root`). Neither Internet Explorer 8 and its lower versions nor the Opera Mini browser supports the `rem` units.

Making your layout fluid

Until now, your layout had a fixed width that was defined by `@basic-width`. A fluid design defines its widths as a percentage of the viewport or the browser window.

To make your layout fluid, define `@basic-width: 900px;` by navigating to `less/responsive/project.less`. After you make the changes, the `@basic-width` variable will be used to set a maximum width instead of a fixed width.

After this, navigate to `less/responsive/mixins responsive.less` in the `.center-content()` mixin and change `width:@basic-width;` to `max-width:@ basic-width;`.

The header will now be fluid, without any further changes. The footer columns are also based on @basic-width, so you will have to change them too.

The width of the footer columns is set by the following code:

```
width: ((@basic-width/3)-@footer-gutter);
```

Change the width of the footer columns in less/responsive/footer.less by using the following code:

```
width: ~"calc((1 / 3 * 100%) - @{footer-gutter})";
```

Instead of the (1 / 3 * 100%) calculation in the preceding code, you can also directly write 33%.

Browser support for the calc() function can be checked by visiting http://caniuse.com/#feat=calc. In addition, remember the note on calc() and the use of string interpolation from *Chapter 1, Improving Web Development with Less*. The Less code is stateless, so these width calculations should be done by CSS in the browser. The browser obtains the real width in pixels the moment the CSS is loaded, so the browser can calculate the column width in pixels and render it.

Finally, you will have to change less/contentresponsive.less and add the media queries to it. If the screen width is lesser than 500 pixels, the navigation and content would be stacked in your layout.

First, make #content and #sidebar fluid by setting their width to width: 2 / 3 * 100%; and width: 1 / 3 * 100%; respectively. Now, the width will be fluid and you can add the media queries. For #content, you should change the code into the following code:

```
width:   2 / 3 * 100%;
float:left;
@media (max-width:500px) {
  width:100%;
  float:none;
}
```

The preceding code sets the width of #content to 100% if the screen width is less than 500 pixels. It also removes the float property of the element so that it will stack as in the original situation. You should do the same for #sidebar.

After these changes for a screen width of 500 pixels, the navigation stacks below the content.

The way in which you can interchange the position of the navigation and content for a screen with a screen width of less than 500 pixels can be seen at `http://localhost/indexresponsivechange.html`. You can accomplish this in two steps. First, interchange the content of `#content` and `#sidebar` inside your HTML document. Open `http://localhost/indexresponsivechange.html` and compare the source code with `http://localhost/indexresponsive.html`. After these changes are made, the sidebar will be visible on the left-hand side of the screen. To move the sidebar to the right, you should set its `float` property to `right` instead of `left`, as shown in the following code:

```
//one third of @basic-width
#sidebar {
  width: 1 / 3 * 100%;
  float:right;
  @media (max-width:500px) {
    width:100%;
    float:none;
  }
}
```

On a small screen, the layout will now look like the following screenshot:

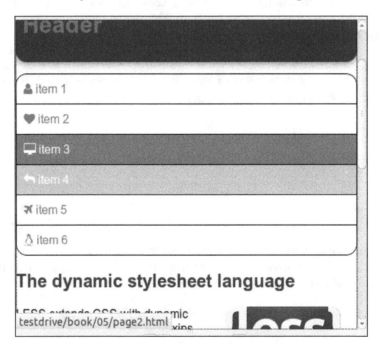

An example of how your layout could look on a mobile phone

Testing your layouts on a mobile phone

It is very likely that you will check your responsive layout on your mobile phone too. Make sure that you add the following additional line of code in the `head` section of your HTML document:

```
<meta name="viewport" content="width=device-width, initial-
  scale=1.0">
```

The preceding code forces the mobile browser to load your website in a viewport that is equal to the screen width of your device. By default, mobile browsers load websites in a viewport that is larger than the screen size. Doing this lets non-mobile websites load similar to how they would on a bigger screen. After loading the website, it's up to the user to scroll and zoom the results. If your optimized mobile layout loads in a viewport with a width that is larger than 500 pixels, the media queries won't work, forcing the viewport to be same as device's screen dimensions and preventing the media query from being applied.

Note that this also means you will have to test this example with a mobile phone that has a screen not wider than 500 pixels. You can also test your designs on websites such as `http://www.responsinator.com/`.

The browser developer tools of modern browsers also have an option to test your designs for different screen widths (which is called the responsive design mode). The following screenshot shows you how the responsive design mode in Firefox looks like:

Responsive design mode in Firefox

Coding first for mobile

Nowadays, it's common to write the styles for mobile devices first and then use media queries to alter them to fit bigger screens. Examples of the **mobile-first** principle of coding can be found in `header.less` and `content.less` from the files of your example layout. In addition, you can open `less/responsive/footer.less` to see how the media query adds the `float` property:

```
@media (min-width:501px) {
  float: left;
  width: ((@basic-width/3)-@footer-gutter);
}
```

This example shows a mobile-first way of coding. Elements stack by default and become horizontal when the screen size grows. Note that older browsers such as Internet Explorer 8 do not support media queries and will always show you the stacked version unless you use a polyfill, such as `Respond.js`. `Respond.js` is a fast and lightweight polyfill for `min-width` or `max-width` CSS3 Media Queries for the Internet Explorer versions before IE9. You can find `Respond.js` at `https://github.com/scottjehl/Respond`.

Using grids in your designs and workflow

The preceding media query example did not use a grid. You may be wondering what a grid is and why you should use it. Grid-based layouts divide your design into a collection of rows with equal-sized columns. Content and graphical elements can be organized according to this layout. Grids help in creating a logical and formal structure for designs. This prevents inconsistencies between the original design and the final implementation in HTML as designers and developers work with the same grid.

Grids are also helpful in responsive design because grid's columns can easily be rearranged to fit different screen widths.

In the previous chapters, you already read about the CSS modules that defined layout structures. Flexboxes and columns can be used to define the CSS layouts and grids. Although these layouts are responsive by default or can be easily defined as responsive, they are not the common way to define your CSS layouts yet. As mentioned earlier, most modern browsers are not ready to support these modules. Luckily, there are alternative ways to define a grid with CSS.

The width of the columns of your grid can be defined as a percentage of the grid or a fixed width. Fluid grids define their widths as a percentage of the viewport. In fluid grids, the column widths vary with the screen width. Fluid layouts can rearrange the content to occupy the available screen width, so the user has to scroll less. On the other hand, designers have less control over the exact representation of the design. For this reason, the majority of responsive grids are a hybrid of fluid and fixed grids.

The role of CSS float in grids

The CSS `float` property is a position property in CSS; the `float` property pushes the elements to the left or right-hand side of the screen and allows other elements to wrap around them. For this reason, the CSS `float` property plays an important role in most CSS grids.

An example will help you understand how this works. Here, you will create a grid with two columns. Let's start writing the Less code for a fixed grid. The example is as follows:

```
@grid-container-width: 940px;
@column-number: 2;

.container {
  width: @grid-container-width;
  .row {
    .col {
      float: left;
      width: (@grid-container-width/@column-number);
    }
    .col2{
      width: 100%;
    }
  }
}
```

You can use the compiled CSS code of the preceding code with the following HTML code:

```
<div class="container">
  <div class="row">
    <div class="col">Column 1</div>
    <div class="col">Column 2</div>
  </div>
  <div class="row">
```

```
        <div class="col2">Column 3</div>
      </div>
   </div>
```

You can inspect the result of the preceding code by visiting `http://localhost/grid.html` from the downloadable example code of this book.

Now, you have an example of a fixed grid. This grid can be made fluid by changing the fixed width using the following Less code:

```
@grid-container-width: 100%;
```

In this grid, the `.container` class holds the grid. This container contains rows (that defined) with the `.row` class. You have to define only two extra classes because this grid has two columns. The first class, `.col`, defines a single column and the second class, `.col2`, defines a double column.

Making your grid responsive

To make grids responsive, you have to define one or more break points. Break points define the screen widths at which a website would respond to provide a suitable layout; below or above the break point, the grid would provide a different layout. In the example grid, you can describe two situations. In the first situation, below the break point (for instance 768 px), the screens will be small. On small screens (keep a mobile phone screen in mind), the columns of the grid should stack. Above the break point, for tablet and desktop screens, the grid will become horizontal and the columns of grid's rows will float next to each other.

In Less, you can write the first situation for small screens using the following code:

```
.container {
  width: @grid-container-width;
  .row {
    .col, .col2 {
      width: 100%;
    }
  }
}
```

All the columns get a width of `100%` of the viewport and none of them float. Starting your code with the smallest screens first, which will generate a mobile-first grid. The mobile-first designs start with a basic design for small screens (and mobile browsers), and they rearrange and add content when the screen size becomes bigger. Note that some mobile browsers don't have full CSS and JavaScript capabilities; these browsers will ignore the advanced features and show your basic design. You are already aware the grid becomes horizontal for larger screens. Other examples can be the navigation, which has got another representation, or an image slider, which is only visible for desktop users.

Now, have a go at making your grid responsive by adding a media query and defining a break point in Less, as shown in the following code:

```less
@break-point: 768px;

.container {
  width: @grid-container-width;
  .row {
    .col, .col2 {
      width: 100%;
    }
    @media(min-width: @break-point) {
      .col {
        float: left;
        width: (@grid-container-width/@column-number);
      }
    }
  }
}
```

The preceding code compiled into the CSS code will look like the following code:

```css
.container {
  width: 100%;
}
.container .row .col,
.container .row .col2 {
  width: 100%;
}
@media (min-width: 768px) {
  .container .row .col {
    float: left;
    width: 50%;
  }
}
```

It's easy to see that now the `.row` classes only float on screens that are wider than 768 pixels. Width columns will stack if the screen size is less than 786 pixels. Open `http://localhost/responsivegrid.html` in your browser to see the preceding responsive code in action.

The role of the clearfix

In the preceding example, columns became horizontal by applying `float:left` to them. The `clearfix()` mixin clears the `float` property of an element after it has been rendered without the need for additional markup, so it can be used for the `.row` classes of the grid. Using these clearfixes guarantees that your elements will only float in their own row.

Using a more semantic strategy

In the previous section, you built a grid using the `div` elements and the CSS classes. Many CSS frameworks, such as Twitter's Bootstrap and ZURB Foundation, construct their grids this way. Critics of the approach claim that it breaks the semantic nature of HTML5. For this reason, they sometimes even compare it with the old-school way of defining layouts with the HTML tables. HTML5 introduces semantic tags, which not only describe the structure but also the meaning of a document. For instance, the `header` tag is semantic; everyone knows what a header is and browsers know how to display them.

Using mixins instead of classes could help you make your grids more semantic.

An example of such a mixin is the following Less code:

```
.make-columns(@number) {
  width: 100%;
  @media(min-width: @break-point) {
    float: left;
    width: (@grid-container-width* ( @number / @grid-columns ));
  }
}
```

The preceding code can be compiled using the following Less code:

```
/* variables */
@grid-columns: 12;
@grid-container-width: 800px;
@break-point: 768px;

header,footer,nav{.make-columns(12);}
```

```
main{.make-columns(8);}
aside{.make-columns(4);}
```

The HTML code for the preceding CSS code will look like the following code:

```
<header role="banner"></header>
<nav role="navigation"></nav>
<main role="main">
  <section></section>
</main>
<aside role="complementary"></aside>
<footer role="contentinfo"></footer>
```

 Note that in the preceding code, @number sets the total width to @number times the width of a column, and the total number of columns in the preceding grid is fixed to be 12.

Building your layouts with grid classes

The .make-columns() mixin can also be used to create your grid classes, as shown in the following code:

```
.make-grid-classes(@number) when (@number>0) {
  .make-grid-classes(@number - 1);
  .col-@{number} {
    .make-columns(@number);
  }
}
.make-grid-classes(12);
```

The preceding code will compile into the following CSS code:

```
.col-1 {
  width: 100%;
}
@media (min-width: 768px) {
  .col-1 {
    float: left;
    width: 66.66666666666666px;
  }
}
.col-2 {
  width: 100%;
```

```
    }
@media (min-width: 768px) {
  .col-2 {
    float: left;
    width: 133.33333333333331px;
  }
}
...
.col-12 {

  width: 100%;

}

@media (min-width: 768px) {

  .col-12 {

    float: left;

    width: 800px;

  }

}
```

In the preceding code, the mixins to build the grid classes are called recursively. You have already seen how to use guards and recursion to construct a loop in *Chapter 3, Nested Rules, Operations, and Built-in Functions*.

Building nested grids

If you set `@grid-container-width` to `100%` and make your grid fluid, the `.make-columns()` mixin can also be used to build nested grids.

Visit `http://localhost/nestedgrid.html` to see an example of such a nested grid.

In HTML, you can write the following code to create a page with the `header`, `content`, `sidebar`, and `footer` properties:

```
<div class="container">
  <header role="banner">header</header>
  <section id="content" role="content">
    <div class="content-column">Column 1</div>
```

```
      <div class="content-column">Column 2</div>
      <div class="content-column">Column 3</div>
   </section>
   <aside role="complementary">sidebar</aside>
   <footer role="contentinfo">footer</footer>
</div>
```

The content property will be divided into three equal-sized columns. To archive the preceding code, you can write the following code in Less:

```
.make-columns(@number) {
  width: 100%;
  @media(min-width: @break-point) {
    float: left;
    width: (@grid-container-width* ( @number / @grid-columns ));
  }
}

/* variables */
@grid-columns: 12;
@grid-container-width: 100%;
@break-point: 768px;

header,footer{.make-columns(12);}
section#content {
  .make-columns(8);
  div.content-column {
    .make-columns(4);
  }
}
#sidebar{.make-columns(4);}
```

Here, the `.make-columns(4);` statement for `div.content-column` will create a width of `33.3%` (4 / 12 * 100%). The 33.3 percent width will be calculated from the direct parent. The direct parent of `div.content-column` is `section#content` in this example. The `section#content` HTML element itself gets a width of 66.6 percent (8 / 12 *100%) of the viewport.

 Note that if you use the preceding grid in your project, you should separate your code into different files. If you create different files for your variables and mixins, your code will be clear and clean.

Alternative grids

In the preceding example, you saw the grid that was defined with columns that become horizontal when the screen size increased. These grids use CSS `float` to align the columns next to each other. In some situations, mostly for older browsers, this may cause some problems in pixel calculation. This problem is sometimes described as the **subpixel rounding** problem. Although `box-sizing: border-box;` will fix the related issues, as described in *Chapter 1, Improving Web Development with Less*, one can choose to use a different grid definition.

CSS isolation provides a solution for this. CSS isolation is not easy to understand. Susy (`http://susydocs.oddbird.net/`) describes it as follows:

> *Every float is positioned relative to its container, rather than the float before it. It's a bit of a hack, and removes content from the flow, so I don't recommend building your entire layout on isolated floats, but it can be very useful as a spot-check when rounding errors are really causing you a headache.*

CSS isolation was originally a part of **Zen Grids** (`http://zengrids.com/`). Zen Grid implementation has been written in SCSS/Sass. It will be relatively easy to rewrite this to Less; you could try this as an exercise. If you want to try this grid system, you can also download some examples of the Less code from `https://github.com/bassjobsen/LESS-Zen-Grid`.

Using the display inline-box

The grid examples that you saw before used the `float` property to build the columns of the grid. Floated elements were displayed next to each other as desired, but they also required clearfixes. The grids also broke the semantic nature of HTML5 in many cases as the grid requires containers that were needed to hold the rows and columns of the grid.

When defining your grid elements as the `inline-box` elements, you can overcome the issues that we just described.

Most HTML elements are `box-level` or `inline` elements by default. You can use the `display` property to change the type of an HTML element. The element type set by the `display` property is part of the CSS visual formatting model and displays an element according to the box model.

Block-level elements start and end with a new line and size up with their parent or take the width and height as defined in HTML or CSS. Inline elements start and end with a white space and size according their content. Inline elements wrap like text on your page. The `div` element is a block-level element while the `span` element is an example of an `inline` element.

Inline-block elements, declared with `display: inline-block`, act like block-level elements and size with their parent, but they start and end with a white space.

Now, you can build a grid with the `inline-block` elements; these elements will be displayed next to each other when allowed by their size and the available space. If an `inline-block` element does not fit on the current line, it will be wrapped to the next line just like a text. Since the `inline-block` elements behave like a text, they have a white space between them. These white spaces can mess up or break your layouts. In addition, the **subpixel rounding** problem may occur when you create layouts with the `inline-block` elements.

The **Justify** grid solves these problems by adding the `text-align: justify` declaration to the grid elements. You can read more about the Justify grid at `http://justifygrid.com/`. The Less code and mixins to build the Justify grids can be downloaded at `https://github.com/CrocoDillon/JustifyGrid/tree/master/Less`.

The Justify grid has 12 columns by default. You can use the mixins of the Justify grid to create a simple, mobile-first, and responsive layout as follows:

```
body {
  #grid;
}
header, footer, section, nav {
  #grid > .cell;
}
@media screen and (min-width: 48em) {
  #grid > .span(4);
}
```

Now, use the preceding Less code with the following HTML structure:

```
<div class="container">
  <header role="banner">header</header>
  <section id="content" role="content">
    <div class="content-column">Column 1</div>
    <div class="content-column">Column 2</div>
    <div class="content-column">Column 3</div>
  </section>
  <aside role="complementary">sidebar</aside>
  <footer role="contentinfo">footer</footer>
</div>
```

Open `http://localhost/justifygrid.html` to see how the preceding code will look in your browser.

Flexbox grids

In *Chapter 1, Improving Web Development with Less*, you read about building layouts with flexible boxes. Internet Explorer 8 does not support flexboxes but almost all other modern browsers do.

Both the grids in the sites, `http://flexboxgrid.com/` and `http://flexible.gs/`, use the `display: flex` declaration, and both the grid systems are compatible with Bootstrap. Bootstrap will be discussed in the next chapter. You can use the flexbox grids with a Bootstrap fallback for the Internet Explorer 8 browser.

The flexbox grid can be found at `http://flexboxgrid.com/`. Currently, this grid does not ship with the Less code, but you can download the Less code from `https://github.com/bassjobsen/flexboxgrid-less`.

A Less plugin for the flexbox grid is also available. You can install this plugin by running the following command in your console:

```
> npm install less-plugin-flexboxgrid
```

After installing the plugin, you can use the grid without importing the flexbox grid library.

Flexible grid system can be found at `http://flexible.gs/`. A Less plugin for this grid system is available too. You can install the plugin for this grid system by running the following command:

```
> npm install less-plugin-flexiblegs
```

Although the CSS3 grid module will possibly replace the flexbox layouts in the future, flexbox layouts have some nice features that you can use now. Flexboxes can be reordered without changing the underlying HTML code. In addition, the vertical alignment of the boxes can be easily set as top, bottom, or center, and the horizontal alignment as start or end.

The flexbox grid mixins create the CSS classes for different features of the `display: flexbox` declaration.

The following HTML code can be used to build a simple responsive layout with the flexbox grid:

```html
<div class="grid">
  <header role="banner">header</header>

  <div class="row">
    <section id="content" role="content" class="col-sm-8">
```

```
      <div class="row reverse middle-sm">
        <div class="col-xs-12 col-sm-4">Column 1<br>second
        line</div>
        <div class="col-xs-12 col-sm-4">Column 2</div>
        <div class="col-xs-12 col-sm-4">Column 3</div>
      </div>
    </section>
    <aside role="complementary" class="col-sm-4">sidebar</aside>
  </div>

  <footer role="contentinfo">footer</footer>
</div>
```

You can inspect the preceding code in your browser by visiting `http://localhost/flexboxgrid.html` from the downloadable source code. The `flexboxgrid.html` file loads the Less code from `less/flexboxgrid/flexbox grid.less`.

The preceding layout will look like that shown in the following screenshot:

header			
Column 3	Column 2	Column 1 second line	sidebar
footer			

A flexbox grid example

As you can see, the content columns are displayed in the reversed order due to the usage of the `reverse` class. In addition, the content in the content columns is vertically aligned in the middle automatically. This is because vertical alignment has been set with the `middle-sm` class.

When compiling your content on the command line, you can also run the following command to compile the flexbox grid classes into your CSS code:

```
> lessc customcode.less styles.css --flexboxgrid
```

Building your project with a responsive grid

In the preceding examples, only the grid columns were defined. This should give you a good and realistic idea of how grids work and how you can use them. A complete grid code will also define responsive containers and row classes. Most grids will also have the so-called **gutters** between their columns. A gutter (which is mostly fixed) is a space that separates the columns of the grid. This also means that a width spanning two columns includes one gutter. Gutters are mostly constructed with the `padding` or `margin` property. If you use the `box-sizing: border-box` setting, which was discussed in *Chapter 1, Improving Web Development with Less*, `padding` should be preferred.

In *Chapter 4, Testing Your Code and Using Prebuilt Mixins Libraries*, you learned how to reuse the Less and prebuilt mixins; you can do the same for grids. It won't be necessary to write the complete code yourself. Frameworks such as Twitter's Bootstrap, Cardinal, flexbox grid, and flexible grid system will provide you with all the Less code and mixins that you need. The flexbox grid and flexible grid system were discussed in the preceding section; you can read more about Bootstrap and Cardinal respectively in *Chapter 6, Using the Bootstrap 3 Frontend Framework*, and *Chapter 7, Less with External Applications and Frameworks*.

Using Preboot's grid system

The following examples will use Preboot's grid mixins to build your project's grid. Finally, you will rebuild the layout example that you used earlier.

Preboot's grid system enables you to build the mobile-first grid layouts with a few variables and mixins. As you saw earlier, you can use Preboot's mixins to create a semantic grid or define more general grid classes.

Preboot defines grid's variables, which are as follows:

```
@grid-columns:         12;
@grid-column-padding:  15px;
@grid-float-breakpoint: 768px;
```

In the preceding code snippet, `@grid-column-padding` defines the width of the gutter, as mentioned earlier. The grid columns are coded with the mobile-first approach. This means that by default they stack vertically and float horizontally when viewport's width is equal to or wider than `@grid-float-breakpoint`. However, let's not forget that `@grid-columns` sets the number of grid columns.

Preboot doesn't provide a container that holds the rows of the grid. You can define this variable yourself to define the maximum width for your grid, as shown in the following code:

```
@grid-width: 960px;
```

There are three available mixins for each part of a standard grid system, which are as follows:

- `.make-row()`: This mixin provides a wrapper for the columns to align their content via a negative margin, and it clear the floats
- `grid.make-column(n)`: This mixin is used to generate n number of columns as a percentage of the available grid columns (that are set via a variable to 12 by default)
- `.make-column-offset(n)`: This mixin pushes a column to the right by n columns via the margin

Now, you can use the preceding variables and mixins with Preboot to make a visible representation of the grid. To begin with, define some grid rows in HTML as follows:

```
<div class="container">
<div class="row">
  <div class="col-12"></div>
</div>
<div class="row">
  <div class="col-11"></div><div class="col-1"></div>
</div>
<div class="row">
  <div class="col-10"></div><div class="col-2"></div>
</div>
<div class="row">
  <div class="col-9"></div><div class="col-3"></div>
</div>
<div class="row">
  <div class="col-6"></div><div class="col-6"></div>
</div>
<div class="row">
  <div class="col-1"></div><div class="col-1"></div><div
    class="col-1"></div><div class="col-1"></div><div class="col-
    1"></div><div class="col-1"></div><div class="col-
    1"></div><div class="col-1"></div><div class="col-
    1"></div><div class="col-1"></div><div class="col-
    1"></div><div class="col-1"></div>
  </div>
</div>
```

The grid used here contains 12 columns and the number of columns in each row should sum up to 12 too.

Now, you can write the the Less code for the preceding grid that makes use of Preboot's mixins and variables. You can again split your code into separate files to keep things clear.

The `project.less` file contains the following Less code that imports all the required files into the project:

```
@import "../normalize.less";
@import "../basics.less";
#preboot { @import (reference) "preboot-master/less/preboot.less";
  }
@import "variables.less";
@import "mixins.less";
@import "grid.less";
@import "styles.less";
```

The `variables.less` file contains the following Less code that defines project's variables:

```
@grid-columns:          12;
@grid-column-padding:   30px;
@grid-float-breakpoint: 768px;
@grid-width: 1200px;
```

The `mixins.less` file contains the mixins for the project as follows:

```
.make-grid-classes(@number) when (@number>0) {

  .make-grid-classes(@number - 1);
  .col-@{number} {
    #preboot > .make-column(@number);
  }
}
```

Note the usage of the `#preboot > .make-column(@number);` namespace here. The loop construct should now look familiar to you.

And, the `grid.less` file contains the following Less code that defines grid's classes:

```
.container {
  max-width: @grid-width;
  padding: 0 @grid-column-padding;
}
```

```
.row {
  #preboot > .make-row()
}
& { .make-grid-classes(12); }
```

The preceding code will create the CSS classes for your grid.

Note that the `.container` class will be used to set the maximum width for the grid. It also sets a padding, which is needed to correct the gutter around the grid. Each row has a padding of half the size of `@grid-column-padding`. The `.containter` class makes the gutter equal to `@grid-column-padding` between two rows, but now, the left and right-hand side of the grid only has a padding that is half the size of `@grid-column-padding`. The `.row` class corrects this by adding a negative margin of half the size of `@grid-column-padding`. Finally, the padding of the container prevents this negative margin from putting the grid off the screen.

Also note the ampersand sign in the `& { .make-grid-classes(12); }` statement. This ampersand sign (which is a reference) guarantees that the inherited `.make-row` mixin will be visible when you need it. The namespaced mixin will not be visible in the global scope. This problem may be fixed in later versions of Less.

And finally, the `styles.less` file contains the following Less code that defines the styles to make the grid columns visible:

```
.row [class^="col-"]{
  background-color: purple;
  height: 40px;
  border: 2px solid white;
}
```

The compiled CSS code from `styles.less` will only be used to make the grid columns visible. As mentioned in *Chapter 1, Improving Web Development with Less,* `[class^="col-"]` is a CSS selector that selects your grid's columns that have a class starting with `col-`, which are your grid's columns. Each column gets a height (`height`), background color (`background-color`), and border (`border`). In addition, the `box-sizing: border-box;` statement here guarantees that the border width will not influence the width of the columns.

You can see the final result by visiting `http://localhost/prebootgridclasses.html` through your browser. The result will look like the following screenshot:

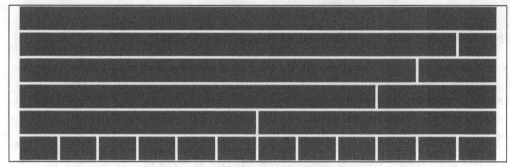

Representation of Preboot's grid with 12 columns

When you see the preceding representation of the grid, you may wonder where the gutters are. As mentioned earlier, the gutters will be constructed with a padding of the columns. You can make them visible by adding some content in the columns. So, try adding the following code to your HTML file:

```
<div class="row">
  <div class="col-6"><p style="background-color:yellow;">make the
    gutter visible</p></div>
  <div class="col-6"><p style="background-color:yellow;">make the
    gutter visible</p></div>
</div>
```

After adding the preceding code to your HTML file, the result will look like the following screenshot:

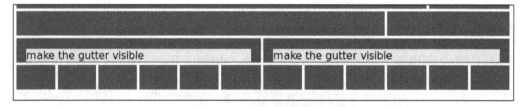

Preboot's grid with 12 columns

The content in the preceding screenshot makes the gutters visible; you will see the gutters of the grid. Also note that the `.col-6` class only has gutters on each side, so the total content width of a `.col-6` class will be six columns, which will include five gutters.

Using the grid mixins to build a semantic layout

In the preceding section, you used Preboot's grid mixins to build grid classes. In the final section of this chapter, you will use these mixins to build a semantic layout.

You can use the same example that we used earlier. Before you start, you should undo the changes made in the examples with media queries. You don't need these media queries here because the grid is responsive by default.

 You can watch the result by visiting `http://localhost/semanticgrid.html`, and you will find the Less files of this example in `/less/semanticgrid/`.

In the current example layout, the container styles are applied to the `body` element. Nowadays, there seems to be no reason to add an extra `div` container (or wrapper). All modern browsers handle the `body` element as a normal block-level element. If you prefer to add an extra wrapper for some reason, please do so. A plausible reason to do so would be, for instance, to add copyrights under your layout; of course, the body doesn't allow you to add something after it. In both cases, this container holds grids' rows.

Open `/less/semanticgrid/project.less` and write the following Less code for the mentioned container into it:

```
body {
  max-width: @basic-width;
  padding: 0 @grid-column-padding;
  margin: 0 auto;
}
```

Note that `@basic-width` in `/less/semanticgrid/variables.less` is set to 900 pixels to make it clear that the grid is responsive with a break point at 768 pixels.

In this semantic example, you will use a grid with only three columns, which is defined in `/less/semanticgrid/variables.less`, using the following code:

```
/* grid */
@grid-columns:          3;
@grid-column-padding:   30px;
@grid-float-breakpoint: 768px;
```

In `/less/semanticgrid/project.less`, you can see that this example doesn't use a namespace for Preboot. The latest version of Less, currently, doesn't support the use of the `namespace` variables in the global scope. In future releases, you can expect `#namespace > @variable` to work, but it doesn't work as of now. Using a `namespace` variable will make the setting of, for instance, `@grid-columns` inside the `namespace` variable from the global scope complex or even impossible.

Now, open `/less/semanticgrid/header.less`. In this file, you can remove the old `.centercontent` class.

Use the `.make-row()` mixin of Preboot to make the `header` tag act like a row and use the `.make-column(3)` mixin call for `h1` inside this `header` tag. The `h1` element will have a width of three columns now.

Do the same for `/less/semanticgrid/content.less` but use `.make-column(2)` for the content and `.make-column(1)` for the sidebar here.

Again, you will see that in the mobile version, the navigation is under the content as explained earlier. You can fix this by using the same trick that you saw earlier in the media queries example. In *Chapter 6, Using the Bootstrap 3 Frontend Framework*, you will learn other ways to solve problems like this. For now, reverse the sidebar and the content in your HTML code so that the sidebar is before the content. After this, you should give the sidebar a `float: right` call, as shown in the following code:

```
@media (min-width: @grid-float-breakpoint) {
  float:right;
}
```

Finally, you have to change the footer. Use `.make-row()` again for the `footer` tag. The `div` elements inside the `footer` tag, which form the columns, will be styled with `.make-column(1)`. After doing this, you will see that footer's columns are shown next to each other without any white space between them. Remember that the gutter of the grid is between the content of the columns and not between the columns itself.

To fix the problem mentioned earlier, apply `background-color`, `border-radius`, and `box-shadow` on the `p` element inside the `div` element, as shown in the following code:

```
div {
.make-column(1);
p {
  min-height: @footer-height;
  background-color: @footer-dark-color;
  //margin: @footer-gutter (@footer-gutter / 2);
  .border-radius(15px);
```

```
  .box-shadow(10px 10px 10px, 70%);
  padding: 10px;
  }
}
```

The preceding code will make the gutter visible, as we saw earlier. The gutter of the grid adds some white space between the columns. There will also be a gutter on the left-hand side of the left column and on the right-hand side of the right column. This will make the total visible width of the footer columns smaller than the header. You can remove these gutters by setting the padding of div to 0 on both the sides. Change the padding on the middle column to give the three columns the same width again. This can be done using the following code:

```
div {

  &:first-child {

    padding-left: 0;

  }

  &:nth-child(2) {

    padding-left: 15px;

    padding-right: 15px;

  }

  &:last-child {

    padding-right: 0;

  }

}
```

Visit http://localhost/semanticgrid.html to see the final result of the preceding code. Resize your browser window to check whether it is indeed responsive.

Extending your grids

In the examples in the preceding section, you used one grid with one break point. Below the break point, your rows simply stack. This seems to work in many cases, but sometimes, it would be useful to have a grid for small screens as well. Imagine you build a photo gallery. On large screens, there will be four photos in a row. But for smaller screens, you don't want the photos to stack; they should be visible as two photos instead of four in a row.

Again, you can resolve this situation by using the grid classes or mixins for a more semantic solution.

In both situations, you should also make your photos responsive. You can do this by adding styles for your images. Setting `max-width` to `100%` and `height` to `auto` does the trick in most cases. The `max-width` variable prevents images from being displayed wider than their original size, and it also ensures that they get 100 percent of their parent's width in other situations. On small screens, these images will get 100 percent width of the viewport.

To make your images responsive by default, you can add the following code to your project's Less code:

```
img {
  display: block;
  height: auto;
  max-width: 100%;
}
```

If you prefer to make your image explicitly responsive by adding a class to each image in your source, you can you use the following Less code to make such a class:

```
.responsive-image {
  display: block;
  height: auto;
  max-width: 100%;
}
```

Adding the grid classes for the small grid

When using the grid classes, you have to change the original `.make-column` mixin from Preboot. This `.make-columns()` mixin sets the styles for a column and adds a media query. The media query in the `.make-columns()` mixin lets the columns to float horizontally for wider viewports. For the new small grid, you don't need a media query because the columns shouldn't be stacked at all.

To accomplish this, you can split the mixin into two new mixins, as shown in the following code:

```
.make-columns(@columns) {
  // Prevent columns from collapsing when empty
  min-height: 1px;
  // Set inner padding as gutters instead of margin
  padding-left: @grid-column-padding;
  padding-right: @grid-column-padding;
  // Proper box-model (padding doesn't add to width)
  .box-sizing(border-box);
}

.float-columns(@columns) {
  float: left;
  // Calculate width based on number of columns available
  width: percentage(@columns / @grid-columns);
}
```

After writing the preceding mixins, you should also create two mixins that will loop to make your grid classes.

The first mixin will look like the following code:

```
.make-grid-columns(@number) when (@number>0) {

  .make-grid-columns(@number - 1);

  .col-small-@{number},.col-large-@{number} {
    .make-columns(@number)
  }
}
```

The preceding mixins will be called from `grid.less` using the `.make-grid-columns(12);` statement. These mixins will be compiled into the following code:

```
.col-small-1,
.col-large-1 {
  min-height: 1px;
  padding-left: 30px;
  padding-right: 30px;
  -webkit-box-sizing: border-box;
  -moz-box-sizing: border-box;
  box-sizing: border-box;
```

```
}
.col-small-2,
.col-large-2 {
  min-height: 1px;
  padding-left: 30px;
  padding-right: 30px;
  -webkit-box-sizing: border-box;
  -moz-box-sizing: border-box;
  box-sizing: border-box;
}
```

After doing this, you can easily see that the preceding code can be optimized to the following code:

```
div[class~="col"] {
  // Prevent columns from collapsing when empty
  min-height: 1px;
  // Set inner padding as gutters instead of margin
  padding-left: @grid-column-padding;
  padding-right: @grid-column-padding;
  // Proper box-model (padding doesn't add to width)
  .box-sizing(border-box);
}
```

The second mixin will look like the following code:

```
.float-grid-columns(@number; @grid-size: large;) when
  (@number>0) {
  .float-grid-columns(@number - 1,@grid-size);
  .col-@{grid-size}-@{number} {
    .float-columns(@number)
  }
}
```

The preceding mixins will be called from grid.less using the following code:

```
.float-grid-columns(12,small);
@media (min-width: @grid-float-breakpoint) {
  .float-grid-columns(12);
}
```

The preceding code will create two sets of grid classes. The large grid classes will only be applied when the media query is `true`. You are perhaps wondering why you can't create these grid classes in one single loop. This is because of the last declaration wins rule; you should define all your large grid classes after the small grid classes. If, for instance, `col-large-2` is defined before `col-small-3`, you can't use `<div class="col-small-3 col-large-2">` because `col-small-3` overrules the styles of `col-large-2`.

After creating your mixins, as described earlier, you can write your HTML code as follows:

```
<div class="row">
  <div class="col-small-6 col-large-3"></div>
  <div class="col-small-6 col-large-3"></div>
  <div class="col-small-6 col-large-3"></div>
  <div class="col-small-6 col-large-3"></div>
</div>
```

The preceding code will show four columns on your screen. These columns will be wider than 768 pixels. The code will also show two columns on smaller screens. You can see an example of this by visiting `http://localhost/prebootgridclassesextend.html`.

Applying the small grid on your semantic code

If you have chosen the semantic way to build your grids, the following example will help you add a small grid to the `footer` section of the layout that you built earlier. You can use the files again by navigating to `/less/semanticgrid/content.less` in this example.

The layout has a break point at 768 pixels. Below this break point, on a small screen, the footer should have three columns; and on big screens, the footer columns should stack.

You can reuse the Preboot mixins that you used earlier in this chapter to build a responsive grid and to create the `footer` columns that we described previously. First, split the mixin into two new mixins: one mixin for floating and one for styling the columns, as shown in the following code:

```
.less-make-column(@columns) {
  float: left;
  // Calculate width based on number of columns available
  width: percentage(@columns / @grid-columns);
```

```
  }
  .iscolumn()
  {
    // Prevent columns from collapsing when empty
    min-height: 1px;
    // Set inner padding as gutters instead of margin
    padding-left: @grid-column-padding;
    padding-right: @grid-column-padding;
    // Proper box-model (padding doesn't add to width)
    .box-sizing(border-box);
  }
```

After creating these mixins, you can use them together with media queries, as follows:

```
  footer {
    .make-row();
    div {
      .iscolumn();
      .less-make-column(1);
      @media (min-width: @grid-float-breakpoint) {
        .less-make-column(3);
      }
    }
  }
```

Summary

You have arrived at the end of this chapter. Hopefully, you feel that you will be able to start your own project with Less. In this chapter, you learned how to use Less for your projects. You also learned how to use media queries and grids to build responsive websites. Now, you are ready to start using Less in your projects. Finally, you will have more time for your real design tasks.

In the next chapter, you will be introduced to Bootstrap. Bootstrap is a popular frontend framework that is commonly used to implement the mobile-first and responsive designs. Bootstrap's CSS code is compiled from Less. You will learn how to use, customize, and extend Bootstrap by using Less for your own projects.

6
Using the Bootstrap 3 Frontend Framework

Bootstrap 3, formerly known as **Twitter's Bootstrap**, is a CSS and JavaScript framework used for building application frontends. The three in Bootstrap 3 refers to the third version of this framework; wherever Bootstrap is mentioned in this book, it refers to its third version. Important changes and improvements have been made to the third version. Bootstrap 3 is not compatible with its earlier versions. Version 4 of Bootstrap will be released in 2015.

Bootstrap 3 can be used for building great frontends. You can download the complete framework, including the Less and JavaScript code, and start using it right away.

This chapter will cover the following topics:

- Bootstrap grids
- Bootstrap's build chain
- Customizing Bootstrap
- Extending Bootstrap
- Theming Bootstrap

Introduction to Bootstrap

Bootstrap provides you with a grid and many other CSS components for building your websites and web applications. You can use the compiled version of Bootstrap directly after downloading it. In this book, you will learn Bootstrap's source code and compile your own version of Bootstrap.

The Less code for compiling Bootstrap's CSS components is well organized. The outcome depends on a set of variables; these variables are grouped in a single `variables.less` file. The lazy loading nature of Less along with the last declaration wins rule enables you to override (or re-declare) these variables later to fit your needs.

Bootstrap also comes with a set of jQuery plugins. Some CSS components depend on these plugins and some Less codes are only needed for these plugins. Modifying or extending the jQuery plugin is beyond of the scope of this book.

The grid, all the other CSS components, and the jQuery plugins are well documented at `http://getbootstrap.com/`.

Bootstrap's default theme looks like the following screenshot:

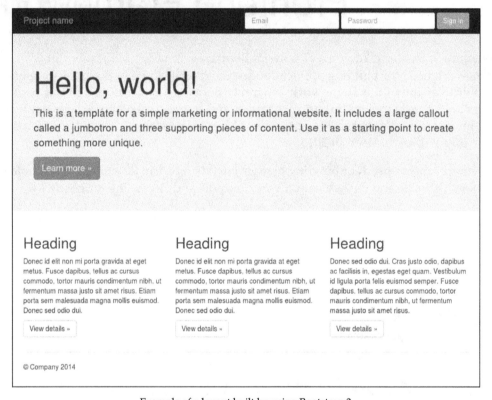

Example of a layout built by using Bootstrap 3

The preceding layout, which uses Bootstrap's jumbotron, can also be found at `http://getbootstrap.com/examples/jumbotron/`.

The time when all Bootstrap websites looked quite similar to each other is gone. Bootstrap will give you all the freedom you need for creating innovative designs.

There is much more to explain about Bootstrap, but for now, let's get back to Less.

The Bootstrap grid

In *Chapter 5*, *Integrating Less in Your Own Projects*, you read about using grids for your designs.

When working with the grid-based layouts, you should arrange your design into a collection of rows with equal-sized columns. Both the developers and the designers use the same grid for building the design, and the grid helps to prevent inconsistencies between the original design and the final implementation of the design in HTML. For responsive layouts, you can reorganize your columns to fit different screen sizes without breaking the design.

Bootstrap has a grid. The grid of Bootstrap is an important feature of the framework, which enables you to build responsive websites and apps with more ease. The grid of Bootstrap is mobile-first by default and has 12 columns. In fact, Bootstrap defines the following four grids in its framework:

- The extra-small grid, which is up to 768 pixels for mobile phones
- The small grid, which is between 768 and 992 pixels for tablets
- The medium grid, which is between 992 and 1200 pixels for desktops
- The large grid, which is 1200 pixels or greater for large desktops

The grids are not completely fluid; depending on the screen size, any one of the four grids can be applied. The four grids have got a fixed width. So, for a screen with a width between 992 and 1200 pixels, the grid will always have a width of 970 pixels.

For the screen widths up to 767 pixels the columns of the grids will be stacked, by default, in a fluid width, and for the larger screen widths the columns will be arranged in a horizontal manner, with a fixed row width. The described mobile-first strategy is implemented by using the CSS media queries, as already discussed in *Chapter 5*, *Integrating Less in Your Own Projects*. The media queries for the grid will look like the code block shown here:

```
/* Extra small devices (phones, less than 768px) */
/* No media query since this is the default in Bootstrap */

/* Small devices (tablets, 768px and up) */
```

```
@media (min-width: @screen-sm-min) { ... }

/* Medium devices (desktops, 992px and up) */
@media (min-width: @screen-md-min) { ... }

/* Large devices (large desktops, 1200px and up) */
@media (min-width: @screen-lg-min) { ... }
```

In *Chapter 5*, *Integrating Less in Your Own Projects*, you learned how to build a grid with the Preboot's mixins. The Bootstrap's grid works in a similar way. Rows have to be placed inside an element (div) with the .container class.

 Note that the .container-fluid class also exists, and you can use this class to create a full-width layout.

The grid rows should have the predefined .row class. The columns in each row can be set in the predefined grid classes. There's a set of 12 grid classes for each of the four grids described earlier: extra small (xs), small (sm), medium (md), and large (lg). The grid classes start with col- followed by the grid shorthand notation (xs, sm, md, and lg), and the number of columns spanned. So, for instance, .col-md-6 spans six columns on a medium grid.

The following HTML code describes a grid element that spans six columns on a small grid and three columns on medium and large grids.

```
<div class="col-sm-6 col-md-3 col-lg-3"></div>
```

Note that the .col-lg-4 class is not required in this situation. The .col-md-4 class will also be applied on the large grid, unless overridden by a .col-lg-* class due to the media queries for the grids that only have a min-width property set. Also, the smallest grid does not require a grid class because the columns in this grid get stacked by default.

You can use the aforementioned grid element to build the following layout:

```
<div class="row">
  <div class="col-sm-6 col-md-3 col-lg-3">1</div>
  <div class="col-sm-6 col-md-3 col-lg-3">2</div>
  <div class="col-sm-6 col-md-3 col-lg-3">3</div>
  <div class="col-sm-6 col-md-3 col-lg-3">4</div>
</div>
```

On small screens, that is, screens with widths between 768 and 992 pixels, the preceding layout will look like the screenshot shown here:

Columns of a small grid

On larger screens, the same code will become horizontal and have 4 columns in a row, as follows:

Columns on a medium and large grid

For screen widths smaller than 768px, the columns will be stacked, as shown here:

Stacked columns on an extra small grid (by default)

Grid variables and mixins

Instead of the predefined grid classes, you can also use Bootstrap as a mixin library to build your own responsive (semantic) grids.

You can use the `.make-row(@gutter: @grid-gutter-width);` mixin to create a wrapper that holds your grid columns together. The following mixins are available to create columns on each of the four grids:

```
.make-xs-column(@columns; @gutter: @grid-gutter-width) {}
.make-sm-column(@columns; @gutter: @grid-gutter-width) {}
.make-md-column(@columns; @gutter: @grid-gutter-width) {}
.make-lg-column(@columns; @gutter: @grid-gutter-width) {}
```

The output of these mixins depends on the variables, as shown here:

```
@grid-columns:          12;
@grid-gutter-width:     30px;
@grid-float-breakpoint: 768px;
```

As an example, consider the following HTML code:

```html
<div class="wrapper">
  <section>content</section>
  <aside>sidebar</aside>
</div>
```

Now the Less code shown here can be used:

```less
@import "bootstrap/less/mixins.less";
@import "bootstrap/less/variables.less";
@import "bootstrap/less/scaffolding.less";

.wrapper {
  .make-row();
}
section {
  .make-sm-column(8);
}
aside {
  .make-sm-column(4);
}
```

The aforementioned code will be compiled into the following CSS code:

```css
.wrapper {
  margin-left: -15px;
  margin-right: -15px;
}
section {
  position: relative;
  min-height: 1px;
  padding-left: 15px;
  padding-right: 15px;
}
@media (min-width: 768px) {
  section {
    float: left;
    width: 66.66666667%;
  }
}
aside {
  position: relative;
  min-height: 1px;
  padding-left: 15px;
```

```
    padding-right: 15px;
  }
  @media (min-width: 768px) {
    aside {
      float: left;
      width: 33.33333333%;
    }
  }
}
```

From the source code of this chapter, you can load `http://localhost/grid.html` on your browser to inspect the results. As you can see, the `section` and `aside` elements are displayed horizontally next to each other for the screen sizes that are wider than 767 pixels.

Note that you don't have to explicitly set the media query declarations when using Bootstrap's mixins and variables for building your grids. Because the mixins follow the mobile-first approach, you should write the code for the mixins for the smallest grid first. This means that you should, for instance, write the `.make-md-column()` mixin before writing the `.make-lg-column()` mixin. This is shown as follows:

```
aside {
  .make-md-column(6);
    .make-lg-column(4);
}
```

Also, note that the `scaffolding.less` file has been imported too. In the `scaffolding.less` file, the `box-sizing` property can be reset by using the code shown here:

```
* {
    .box-sizing(border-box);
}
*:before,
*:after {
    .box-sizing(border-box);
}
```

You can read about the `box-sizing` property and how resetting the `box-sizing` property helps in simplifying the grid calculations in *Chapter 1, Improving Web Development with Less*.

Working with Bootstrap's Less files

All of the CSS code for Bootstrap is written in Less. You can download Bootstrap's Less files and recompile your own version of the CSS code. The Less files can be used to customize, extend, and reuse Bootstrap's code. In the next sections, you will learn how to do this.

 To download the Less files, visit `http://getbootstrap.com/`. To visit Bootstrap's GitHub pages, go to `https://github.com/twbs/bootstrap`. On this page, click on **Download Zip** on the right-hand side column for the latest version of the framework. Alternatively, you can download the source code from `http://getbootstrap.com/getting-started/#download`. This will give you the latest stable version.

The source code includes the Less files too.

Building a Bootstrap project with Grunt

After downloading the files mentioned earlier, you can build a Bootstrap project with Grunt. Grunt is a JavaScript task runner; it can be used for the automation of your processes. Grunt helps you when performing repetitive tasks, such as minifying, compiling, unit testing, and linting your code.

Grunt runs on `node.js` and uses `npm`, which you have used earlier, while installing the Less compiler. Node.js is a standalone JavaScript interpreter built on Google's V8 JavaScript runtime, as used in Chrome. It can be used for easily building fast and scalable network applications. You can read more about `node.js` in the book, *Node Cookbook: Second Edition, David Mark Clements, Packt Publishing*, which can be found at `https://www.packtpub.com/web-development/node-cookbook-second-edition`. If you have not installed `node.js` on your system yet, you can visit `https://nodejs.org/download/` to find out how to install it. Node.js comes with `npm`, so when you install `node.js`, `npm` will be installed with it.

When you unzip the files from the downloaded file, you will find `Gruntfile.js` and `package.json`, among other files. The `package.json` file contains the metadata for the projects published as the `npm` modules. The `Gruntfile.js` file is used to configure or define tasks and load the Grunt plugins. The Bootstrap Grunt configuration is a great example for showing you how to set up a build chain, including automation testing for projects. The build chain of Bootstrap handles the HTML, Less (CSS), and JavaScript code. This book can't discuss all of this; more information about `Grunt.js` can be found in the book, *Grunt.js Cookbook: RAW, Jurie-Jan Botha*, which is available at `http://www.packtpub.com/grunt-js-cookbook/book`. The parts that are interesting for you as a Less developer are discussed in this chapter.

In `package.json` file, you will find that Bootstrap compiles its Less files with `grunt-contrib-less`. The configuration for `grunt-contrib-less` will look like the code block shown here:

```
less: {
  compileCore: {
    options: {
      strictMath: true,
      sourceMap: true,
      outputSourceFiles: true,
      sourceMapURL: '<%= pkg.name %>.css.map',
      sourceMapFilename: 'dist/css/<%= pkg.name %>.css.map'
    },
    src: 'less/bootstrap.less',
    dest: 'dist/css/<%= pkg.name %>.css'
  }
}
```

In the aforementioned code, `compileCore` is a subtask. A second subtask called `compileTheme` compiles a single theme CSS file. Bootstrap does not use the Less `clean-css` and the `autoprefix` plugin to optimize and `autoprefix` the compiled code. Instead of the Less plugins, different tasks for the postprocess are used.

Apart from `grunt-contrib-less`, and the postprocess `clean-css` plugin, and the `autoprefix` tasks, Bootstrap also uses `grunt-contrib-csslint` to check the compiled CSS for syntax errors. The `grunt-contrib-csslint` plugin also helps improve browser compatibility, performance, maintainability, and accessibility. The plugin's rules are based on the principles of object-oriented CSS (`http://www.slideshare.net/stubbornella/object-oriented-css`). You can find out more about it by visiting `https://github.com/stubbornella/csslint/wiki/Rules`.

Bootstrap makes heavy use of the Less variables. You will find these variables in `less/variables.less`. These variables can also be set by the customizer. The customizer can be found at `http://getbootstrap.com/customize/`. Note that the customizer only generates the compiled CSS code and does not deliver a modified `less/variables.less` file. When you begin to modify and extend Bootstrap as described in this chapter, you should not use the customizer. You should edit the Less code directly.

Whoever has studied the source of `Gruntfile.js` may very well have found a reference to the `BsLessdocParser` Grunt task. This Grunt task is used to build Bootstrap's customizer dynamically based on the Less variables used by Bootstrap. The process of parsing the Less variables to build, for instance, Bootstrap's documentation will be very interesting; however, this task is not discussed in this book.

Last but not the least, let's have a look at the basic steps required to run Grunt from the command line and build Bootstrap. Grunt will be installed with npm. The npm package checks Bootstrap's package.json file and automatically installs the necessary local dependencies listed there.

To build Bootstrap with Grunt, you will have to enter the following commands on the command line:

```
> npm install -g grunt-cli
> cd /path/to/extracted/files/bootstrap
> npm install
```

After this, you can compile the CSS and JavaScript code by running the following command:

```
> grunt dist
```

This command will compile your files into the /dist directory. The > grunt test command will also run the built-in tests.

Now, you can modify less/variables.less and compile your own version of Bootstrap. Note that changing less/variables.less directly will hinder updating the code. In this chapter, you will learn how to modify and extend Bootstrap, while leaving the original code files untouched.

You can use both npm and bower to keep your source files up-to-date. Bootstrap can be installed along with npm by simply running the following command:

```
> npm install bootstrap
```

The preceding command will install Bootstrap's code files into the lnode_modules folder.

Bower is a package manager for frontends. You can use Bower to keep your source code up-to-date. You can install bower by running the command shown here:

```
> npm install -g bower
```

After installing bower, you can install Bootstrap as follows:

```
> bower install bootstrap
```

The preceding command installs Bootstrap in the bower_components directory.

When you have installed Bootstrap with `npm` or `bower`, you can import `less/bootstrap.less` into your project so as to use it for further customizations. Note that you can re-declare all the variables defined in `less/variables.less` afterwards, thanks to the lazy loading nature of Less.

When you use Bower for package management, you should also take a look at the Less Bower `resolve` plugin. This plugin can be installed by using the following command:

```
> npm install less-plugin-bower-resolve
```

Without this plugin, you will have to use the following code for importing a module.

```
@import "bower_components/my-module/src/hello.less";
@import "bower_components/my-module/src/world.less";
```

When using this plugin, you have to only write `@import "my-module"`. The preceding code requires that `bower_components/my_module/bower.json` contains the lines of code as shown here:

```
{
  "main": [
    "src/hello.less",
    "src/world.less"
  ]
}
```

Autoprefixing your code

Since the advent of Version 3.2, Bootstrap has integrated the Grunt `autoprefix` plugin into its build chain. When you compile Bootstrap without using the Grunt tools, you should integrate the autoprefixing yourself. This is done to compile the CSS code that supports the same range of browsers as Bootstrap does.

When compiling your code on the command line, you can use the Less `autoprefix` plugin. After running `npm install less-plugin-autoprefix` on the command line, you can use the `--autoprefix` option with the `lessc` command. The `--autoprefix` option will enable you to specify a comma-separated list of the target browsers.

The target browsers used by the current version of Bootstrap can be found in the `configBridge.json` file of Bootstrap's source code.

Now, you can run the following command:

```
lessc bootstrap.less bootstrap.css --autoprefix="Android 2.3,Android >=
4,Chrome >= 20,Firefox >= 24,Explorer >= 8",iOS >= 6,Opera >= 12,Safari
>= 6"
```

Compiling your Less files

Although you can build Bootstrap with Grunt, you don't have to use it. You will find the Less files in a separate directory called `/less` inside the root `/bootstrap` directory. The main project file is `bootstrap.less`; other files will be covered in the next section. You can use `bootstrap.less` in the same way as you have done in the earlier chapters.

You can include `bootstrap.less` with `less.js` into your HTML code for the purpose of testing as shown here:

```
<link rel="bootstrap/less/bootstrap.less" type="text/css"
  href="less/styles.less" />
<script type="text/javascript">less = { env: 'development'
  };</script>
<script src="less.js" type="text/javascript"></script>
```

Of course, you can also compile this file server side as follows:

```
lessc bootstrap.less  bootstrap.css
```

Both of the methods described here do not use the CSS vendor prefix in the code. You should use the Less `autoprefix` plugin, as described in the previous section, when compiling the code on the command line. The `autoprefix` plugin won't work when compiling the code in a browser. The `Prefixfree` JavaScript library can be used for compiling the code in a browser. When compared to Bootstrap, the `Prefixfree` library does not support the same range of browsers. You can find the `Prefixfree` library at http://lea.verou.me/prefixfree/.

Bootstrap Less plugin

The Bootstrap Less plugin can be installed by running the following command:

```
npm less-plugin-bootstrap
```

You can only use this plugin when compiling the code on the command line. When you use this plugin, the Bootstrap Less code will be imported before the custom code. The preceding command means that you can use Bootstrap without explicitly importing the Less code of Bootstrap.

Note that the plugin does not reference the source files but imports them normally, so all of the Bootstrap's code will be compiled in the final CSS code.

The following example will show you how to use this plugin. **Bootswatch** provides free themes for Bootstrap. You can download these themes from `http://bootswatch.com/`. Each theme comes with a `variables.less` file and a `bootswatch.less` file. In the `bootswatch` folder of the downloaded source code, you will find the Less files for the Cerulean theme. After downloading the files, you can create a project file as shown here:

```
@import "variables.less";
@import "bootswatch.less";
```

Now, you can compile the theme by using the following command on your console:

```
lessc project.less  project.css --bootstrap
```

After compiling the Less code, you can visit `http://localhost/bootswatch/index.html` for downloading the source code in your browser. You will see that the `jumbotron` template we used before will look quite different after applying the Cerulean theme.

Diving into Bootstrap's Less files

Now it's time to look at Bootstrap's Less files in more detail. The `/less` directory contains a long list of files. You will recognize some files by their names. You have seen files such as `variables.less`, `mixins.less`, and `normalize.less` earlier. Open `bootstrap.less` to see how the other files are organized. The comments inside `bootstrap.less` tell you that the Less files are organized by functionality, as shown in the following code snippet:

```
// Core variables and mixins
// Reset
// Core CSS
// Components
```

Although Bootstrap is strongly CSS-based, some of the components don't work without the related JavaScript plugins. The `navbar` component is an example of this. Bootstrap's plugins require jQuery. You can't use the newest 2.x version of jQuery, because this version doesn't have support for Internet Explorer 8.

To compile your own version of Bootstrap, you have to change the variables defined in `variables.less`. In previous chapters, you learned that you don't have to overwrite the original files and variables. When using the last declaration wins and lazy loading rules, re-declaring some variables will be easy. Re-declaration of variables was discussed in *Chapter 2, Using Variables and Mixins*.

Creating a custom button with Less

By default, Bootstrap defines seven different buttons, as shown in the following screenshot:

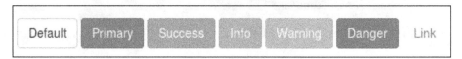

The seven different button styles of Bootstrap 3

Take a look at the HTML structure of Bootstrap's buttons shown here before you start writing the Less code.

```
<!-- Standard button -->
<button type="button" class="btn btn-default">Default</button>
```

A button has two classes. Globally, the first `.btn` class provides the layout styles, and the second `.btn-default` class adds the colors. In this example, you will only change button's colors, and its layout will be kept as it is.

Open `buttons.less` in your text editor. In this file, you will find that the following Less code has been used for the different buttons:

```
// Alternate buttons
// --------------------------------------------------
.btn-default {
  .button-variant(@btn-default-color; @btn-default-bg;
    @btn-default-border);
}
```

The preceding code makes it clear that you can use the `.button-variant()` mixin to create the customized buttons. For instance, to define a custom button, you can use the following Less code:

```
// Customized colored button
// --------------------------------------------------
.btn-colored {
  .button-variant(blue;red;green);
}
```

In the preceding case, you want to extend Bootstrap with your customized button, add your code to a new file, and call this `custom.less` file. Appending `@ import custom.less` to the list of components inside `bootstrap.less` will work well. The disadvantage of this is that you will have to change `bootstrap.less` again when updating Bootstrap. So, alternatively, you could create a file, such as `custombootstrap.less`, which contains the following code:

```
@import "bootstrap.less";
@import "custom.less";
```

The previous step extends Bootstrap with a custom button. Alternatively, you could change the colors of the default button by re-declaring its variables. To do this, create a new file, `custombootstrap.less`, and then add the code shown here to it:

```
@import "bootstrap.less";
//== Buttons
//
//## For each of Bootstrap's buttons, define text, background and
border color.
@btn-default-color:          blue;
@btn-default-bg:             red;
@btn-default-border:         green;
```

In some situations, you will, for instance, need to use the button styles without using anything else of Bootstrap. In these situations, you can use the `reference` keyword with the `@import` directive, as discussed in *Chapter 5, Integrating Less in Your Own Projects*.

You can use the following Less code for creating a Bootstrap button for the project:

```
@import (reference) "bootstrap.less";
.btn:extend(.btn){};
.btn-colored {
  .button-variant(blue;red;green);
}
```

You can see the result of the preceding code by visiting `http://localhost/button. html`.

 Note that depending on the version of `less.js`, you may find some unexpected classes in the compiled output. Sometimes, media queries or extended classes break the referencing in the older versions of `less.js`.

Customizing Bootstrap's navbar with Less

An important component of Bootstrap is the navigation bar. The navigation bar adds the main navigation to a website. It mostly contains a logo or a brand name, a searchbox, and a few navigation links. In this book, navbar refers to the navigation bar. A typical Bootstrap navbar component will look like the following screenshot:

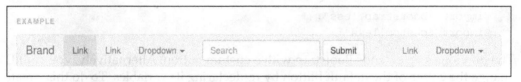

Example of a Bootstrap navbar component

Bootstrap's navbar component is responsive by default. On small screen sizes, the preceding navbar component will look like the following screenshot:

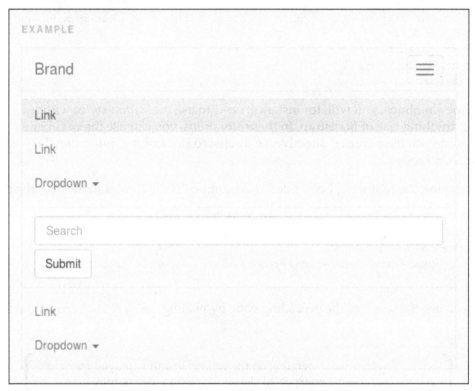

A collapsed and opened Bootstrap navbar component

In addition to the CSS code, Bootstrap's responsive `navbar` component requires the `collapse` JavaScript plugin. This plugin should be included in your version of Bootstrap. By default, the build chain of Bootstrap bundles all the JavaScript plugins in to a single line. You can find these files in `dist/js`. You can use the following HTML code for including Bootstrap's plugin in your document:

```
<!-- jQuery (necessary for Bootstrap's JavaScript plugins) -->
<script
  src="https://ajax.googleapis.com/ajax/libs/jquery/1.11.2/
    jquery.min.js"></script>
<!-- Include all compiled plugins (below), or include individual files
as needed -->
<script src="dist/js/bootstrap.min.js"></script>
```

As the plugins require jQuery, you should include jQuery. Instead of `dist/js/bootstrap.min.js`, you can also include the individual files. The plugins can be found in the `/js` folder of the source code. Alternatively, comment out the plugin you do not need in the the `Gruntfile.js` file, and compile your own custom version of the `bootstrap.js` file.

Now try to change the colors of the default `navbar` component. To do this, you must first open `variables.less` to find out which variables color the `navbar` component, as shown here:

```
//== Navbar
//
//##

// Basics of a navbar
@navbar-height:                    50px;
@navbar-margin-bottom:             @line-height-computed;
@navbar-border-radius:             @border-radius-base;
@navbar-padding-horizontal:        floor((@grid-gutter-width /
  2));
@navbar-padding-vertical:          ((@navbar-height -
  @line-height-computed) / 2);
@navbar-collapse-max-height:       340px;

@navbar-default-color:             #777;
@navbar-default-bg:                #f8f8f8;
@navbar-default-border:            darken(@navbar-default-bg,
  6.5%);

// Navbar links
@navbar-default-link-color:              #777;
```

```
@navbar-default-link-hover-color:        #333;
@navbar-default-link-hover-bg:           transparent;
@navbar-default-link-active-color:       #555;
@navbar-default-link-active-bg:          darken(@navbar-default-
   bg, 6.5%);
@navbar-default-link-disabled-color:     #ccc;
@navbar-default-link-disabled-bg:        transparent;

// Navbar brand label
@navbar-default-brand-color:             @navbar-default-link-
   color;
@navbar-default-brand-hover-color:       darken(@navbar-default-
   brand-color, 10%);
@navbar-default-brand-hover-bg:          transparent;

// Navbar toggle
@navbar-default-toggle-hover-bg:         #ddd;
@navbar-default-toggle-icon-bar-bg:      #888;
@navbar-default-toggle-border-color:     #ddd;
```

You have seen that it was easy to find these variables. The comments in the file are a handy guide for finding them. You will also see that the meaningful and descriptive names for the variables make sense, as learned in *Chapter 2, Using Variables and Mixins*. On the other hand, you may be wondering why so many variables are there for the navbar component. The navbar component has many elements and many manifestations that need to be defined by variables. As mentioned earlier, Bootstrap's navbar component is responsive by default; it collapses for smaller screens (or in fact, from the mobile-first point of view, it becomes horizontal for the larger screen sizes). So, styles must be defined for both the collapsed and horizontal versions of the navbar component. Colors for the navbar links and the collapsed menu toggle button are also set in the preceding code.

Just like Bootstrap's buttons, the Bootstrap navbar component is also built by using two classes, as shown in the following code snippet:

```
<nav class="navbar navbar-default" role="navigation"></nav>
```

In this case, the .navbar class provides the layout styles, and the second .navbar-default class adds the colors and other variations. The .navbar class has a third class that sets its type. There are four types of navbar class: the default, fixed to top, fixed to bottom, and static top classes.

The navbar classes can be found in navbar.less. The navbar class doesn't have a mixin for building the classes. The Less code provides classes for two alternate navbar styles, .navbar-default and .navbar-inverse.

As there are no mixins to be used here, re-declaration of some of the navbar class' variables will be the best option for customizing its look and feel. Alternatively, you can copy the complete .navbar-default class and use it for customization. Bootstrap intends to use only one navbar component per page, so the additional style classes don't have any added value.

For instance, set the color using the following code:

```
@navbar-default-color:        red;
@navbar-default-bg:           blue;
@navbar-default-border:       yellow;
```

You can declare these variables as customnavbar.less and also add @import "bootstrap.less"; to this file. Now you can compile customnavbar.less.

You can see the result of the preceding code by visiting http://localhost/customnavbar.html.

At the end of the file, you will also find the following code:

```
<!-- jQuery (necessary for Bootstrap's JavaScript plugins) -->
<script
  src="https://ajax.googleapis.com/ajax/libs/jquery/1.11.2/
    jquery.min.js"></script>
<!-- Include all compiled plugins (below), or include individual
  files as needed -->
<!-- Latest compiled and minified JavaScript -->
<script
  src="https://maxcdn.bootstrapcdn.com/bootstrap/3.3.2/js/
    bootstrap.min.js"></script>
```

This code is needed because the responsive navbar class requires the collapse plugin.

Bootstrap classes and mixins

When skipping through the components, you will see that Bootstrap is a complete framework. After the compilation of the framework, you should have all the classes you need for building your responsive website. On the other hand, Bootstrap can also be used as a library. You have already seen how to use only buttons.

In utilities.less, you can find the code as shown here:

```
.clearfix {
  .clearfix();
}
```

The preceding code makes the `.clearfix` class available for direct usage in the HTML code; on the other hand, you can still reuse the `.clearfix()` mixin. Note that the `.clearfix()` mixin itself can be found in `mixins/clearfix.less`.

You can find Bootstrap's mixins in the `mixins` folder. The `mixins.less` file imports all these files into your project. The `mixins.less` file contains some comments too. These comments describe the usage of the mixins. The mixins, in `vendorprefixes.less`, have deprecated in v3.2.0 due to the introduction of the autoprefixer in the Grunt build chain. These mixins will be removed in the Version 4 of Bootstrap.

This strict separation of mixins and classes allows you to import the mixins and apply these mixins to your code under your class name(s), without actually creating an output for these classes. The preceding import of the `mixins.less` file will allow you to use Bootstrap's gradient mixins for your projects, as shown in the following code snippet:

```
@import "bootstrap/mixins.less";
header {
  #gradient > .horizontal(red; blue);
}
```

The preceding code will be compiled into the CSS code shown here:

```
header {
  background-image: -webkit-linear-gradient(left,
    color-stop(#ff0000 0%), color-stop(#0000ff 100%));
  background-image: linear-gradient(to right, #ff0000 0%, #0000ff
    100%);
  background-repeat: repeat-x;
  filter:
    progid:DXImageTransform.Microsoft.gradient
      (startColorstr='#ffff0000', endColorstr='#ff0000ff',
        GradientType=1);
}
```

As you can see, the `gradient` mixins are namespaced. Visit `http://localhost/gradient.html` to see how the background gradient explained in the preceding example looks.

You will find the Less code for each component and plugin in a single file, in the
`less` directory. Mixins used in these files are stored in the mixin directory, according
to the same naming conventions. So, the code for the progress bars component can be
found in `less/progress-bars.less`. This file calls mixins, such as the `.progress-bar-variant()` mixin. You will find the `.progress-bar-variant()` mixin, as
expected, in `less/mixins/progress-bars.less`. In most cases, the code also
depends on mixins or variables not directly related to the component. The progress
bar's code also requires the `gradient` mixins.

To compile the code for a single component, you can import the complete Bootstrap
Less code with the `reference` keyword as shown earlier. Alternatively, you can
import variables and mixins. Both variables and mixins do not give an output to the
compiled CSS code. The code for a progress bar, as described in the preceding code
snippet, can look like the following code block:

```
@import "variables.less";
@import "mixins.less";
@import (reference) "progress-bars.less";
.progress:extend(.progress){};
.progress-bar:extend(.progress-bar){};
.custom-progress-bar {
  .progress-bar-variant(black);
}
```

The aforementioned Less code will output the following CSS code:

```
.progress {
  overflow: hidden;
  height: 20px;
  margin-bottom: 20px;
  background-color: #f5f5f5;
  border-radius: 4px;
  -webkit-box-shadow: inset 0 1px 2px rgba(0, 0, 0, 0.1);
  box-shadow: inset 0 1px 2px rgba(0, 0, 0, 0.1);
}
.progress-bar {
  float: left;
  width: 0%;
  height: 100%;
  font-size: 12px;
  line-height: 20px;
  color: #ffffff;
  text-align: center;
```

```
    background-color: #337ab7;
    box-shadow: inset 0 -1px 0 rgba(0, 0, 0, 0.15);
    transition: width 0.6s ease;
}

.custom-progress-bar {
    background-color: blue;
}
.progress-striped .custom-progress-bar {
    background-image: linear-gradient(45deg, rgba(255, 255, 255,
        0.15) 25%, transparent 25%, transparent 50%, rgba(255, 255,
        255, 0.15) 50%, rgba(255, 255, 255, 0.15) 75%, transparent
            75%, transparent);
}
```

In the preceding code, the `reference` keyword was used when importing the
`progress-bars.less` file. The `progress-bars.less` file also outputs Bootstrap's
default progress bars. The `reference` keyword prevents unused output, but should
be used with care. Progress bars, just like buttons and panels, require two CSS
classes: the main class (`.progress-bar`) and the style class (`.custom-progress-
bar`). To generate the base class, the `.progress-bar:extend(.progress-bar){}`;
code has been used. That's not all, because the progress bars should also be wrapped
in an element with the `.progress` class. So, the `.progress:extend(.progress){}`;
line is also required when referencing.

Now the compiled code can be used with the HTML code, as shown here:

```
<div class="progress">
  <div class="progress-bar custom-progress-bar" role="progressbar"
    aria-valuenow="45" aria-valuemin="0" aria-valuemax="100"
      style="width: 45%">
    <span class="sr-only">45% Complete</span>
  </div>
</div>
```

The progress bar will now look like the following screenshot:

45% Complete

Custom black Bootstrap progress bar

For the stripped variant of the progress bar, you should also compile the `.progress-
bar-striped:extend(.progress-bar-striped){}`; code. The `.progress-
striped .custom-progress-bar` selector compiled here was deprecated in v3.2.0
of Bootstrap.

The stripped variant of the progress bars should look like the following screenshot:

Custom stripped black Bootstrap progress bar

Finally, Bootstrap has an animated variant of the stripped progress bar. Even after you compile the .active class into the CSS code with the following code, the CSS code you have compiled will still miss the required @keyframes declaration for the animation:

```
.custom-progress-bar {
  .progress-bar-variant(black);
  &.active {
    &:extend(.progress-bar.active);
  }
}
```

So, in case you want to compile your custom progress bar with animation, you should consider not using the reference.

You can open http://localhost/customprogressbars.html to see how the custom progress bars appear. You can also open http://localhost/customprogressbarsactive.html to see an animated custom progress bar. The customprogressbarsactive.html file compiles the customprogressbarsactive.less file; this file does not reference the code in boostrap/less/progress-bars.less. The content of the customprogressbarsactive.less file will look as shown here:

```
@import "bootstrap/less/variables.less";
@import "bootstrap/less/mixins.less";
@import "bootstrap/less/progress-bars.less";
.custom-progress-bar {
  .progress-bar-variant(purple);
}
```

Theming Bootstrap with Less

As Bootstrap's styles are built with Less, it will be easy to theme your own version of Bootstrap. There are basically two ways of integrating your theme's Less code.

The first method compiles all the code into a single CSS file. This method is recommended in most cases, because loading requires only one HTTP request.

To use this method, import your theme file into `bootstrap.less` with the `@import` statement and recompile Bootstrap. Alternatively, create a new project file, for instance, `bootstraptheme.less`, which includes both of those, as shown in the following code snippet:

```
@import "bootstrap.less";
@import "theme.less";
```

This method overwrites Bootstrap's styles at the Less level, while the second method does the same at the CSS level. In the second method, the theme's Less code will be compiled into separate CSS files, which will be loaded after Bootstrap's CSS.

Your HTML code for client-side compiling will be as shown here:

```
<link rel="stylesheet/less" type="text/css"
  href="less/bootstrap/bootstrap.less" />
<link rel="stylesheet/less" type="text/css"
  href="less/yourtheme.less" />
<script type="text/javascript">less = { env: 'development'
  };</script>
<script src="less.js" type="text/javascript"></script>
```

Your HTML code after the server-side compiling will be as follows:

```
<link type="text/css"  rel="stylesheet"
  href="css/bootstrap.min.css" />
<link type="text/css"  rel="stylesheet"
  href="css/yourtheme.min.css" />
```

The second method requires an extra HTTP request when loading your page, but it offers the opportunity to load Bootstrap's core from CDN as shown here:

```
<link type="text/css"  rel="stylesheet"
  href="//netdna.bootstrapcdn.com/bootstrap/3.1.1/css/
    bootstrap.min.css" />
<link type="text/css" rel="stylesheet"
  href="css/yourtheme.min.css" />
```

The a11y theme for Bootstrap

A11y is a commonly used shorthand for (web) accessibility. Accessibility plays an important role in modern web design. Nevertheless, many websites pay less attention to it. The a11y theme for Bootstrap provides better accessibility to Bootstrap.

The a11y theme can be downloaded from `https://github.com/bassjobsen/ bootstrap-a11y-theme`. You only have to compile the Less file to use the theme. Also, in this case, you can choose between integrating the Less code into your Less code base and compiling a separate theme's CSS file.

For more accessibility and improvements of Bootstrap, take a look at `https:// github.com/paypal/bootstrap-accessibility-plugin/`. Note that this plugin doesn't provide any Less code, but only the CSS code.

Color schemes with 1pxdeep

1pxdeep helps you in using relative visual weight and color schemes in your project. Based on a seed color, 1pxdeep's `scheme.less` file generates a color palette with 16 colors. Each color is also defined by a variable. The variables, such as `@color1` or `@ color4c`, can be used for the customization of your design. Every color variable also defines a class with the same name, so `@color1` in your Less code and `.color1` in your HTML code will refer to the same color in your color scheme.

After implementing 1pxdeep in your project, changing the branding or coloring scheme will be as simple as changing the seed color.

A typical Less project file using 1pxdeep and Bootstrap will look like the following code snippet:

```
@import "scheme.less"; // color scheme
@import "bootstrap.less"; // bootstrap
@import "1pxdeep.less"; // 1pxdeep theme
@import "style.less"; // your own styles
```

The preceding code re-declares Bootstrap's variables, such as `@brand-primary: hsl(hue(#428bca),@sat,@l-factor);`, and enables you to use 1pxdeep's variables, such as `@color3` in the `style.less` file, as shown here:

```
header {
  background-color: @color3;
  h1 {
    color: @color3a;
  }
}
```

1pxdeep's CSS classes can also be used directly in the HTML code as follows:

```
<button class="btn btn-default color1">Color 1</button>
```

On 1pxdeep's website, you can test the different seed colors to get an impression of how they look. Visit `http://rriepe.github.io/1pxdeep/`.

Summary

In this chapter, you learned how to use Less with Bootstrap. You can now build a customized version of Bootstrap with ease. You also learned how to extend Bootstrap and reuse its code. The Less code of Bootstrap is well organized, and it can be a great example for starting your own project or for creating your own mixins library.

In the next chapter, you will read about the other frameworks and grid systems, which can be build with Less. You will also learn to integrate and use Less with the other applications and frameworks.

7

Less with External Applications and Frameworks

After reading the previous chapters, you should have learned enough to build your own projects with Less. You will write better CSS and achieve more success at the same time. Now, you are definitely ready to learn the last step. In this chapter, you will learn how to use Less with the other well-known frameworks, applications, and tools. You will read about the web developer's tools that are built with Less or have integrated Less in their workflow. These projects can be used, customized, and extended with Less and will help you build better projects with Less.

In this chapter, we will cover the following topics:

- Cardinal CSS
- Ionic framework and Less
- Semantic UI
- Building grids with Less
- WordPress and Less
- Using Less with the Play framework, AngularJS, Meteor, and Rails
- Alternative compilers for compiling your Less code

Cardinal CSS

In the preceding chapter, you learned how to build frontends with Bootstrap. Also, Cardinal is also a CSS framework. It is mobile-first and modular; unlike Bootstrap, it is a pure CSS framework without any JavaScript plugins. Of course, Cardinal's CSS has been written with Less. It offers a flexible grid system and encapsulated styles for the common UI objects. You can read more about it and download Cardinal at http://cardinalcss.com/.

Although the framework works well, it lacks documentation. In the Less code itself, you will find useful comments. With all the knowledge that you gained by reading this book, you should be able to use these comments to build a frontend with Cardinal.

The HTML code for a grid can look like the following code block:

```
<div class="grid">
  <div class="grid-item one-whole md-one-half
    xl-one-fourth">1</div>
  <div class="grid-item one-whole md-one-half
    xl-one-fourth">2</div>
  <div class="grid-item one-whole md-one-half
    xl-one-fourth">3</div>
  <div class="grid-item one-whole md-one-half
    xl-one-fourth">4</div>
</div>
```

The grids of Cardinal have 12 columns by default. As can be seen in the preceding code, Cardinal uses descriptive names for the predefined grid classes. The .lg-1/4 class can be used instead of the .lg-one-fourth class, both classes span across three columns.

Note that Cardinal has seven grids with six breakpoints, which are defined as shown in the following code:

```
@screen-xs:  480px;
@screen-sm:  600px;
@screen-md:  768px;
@screen-lg:  960px;
@screen-xl:  1140px;
@screen-xxl: 1380px;
```

The Less Cardinal plugin

The Less plugin for Cardinal automatically imports Cardinal's Less code before the custom code. You can install this plugin by running the following command on the console:

```
> npm install less-plugin-cardinal
```

The build chain of Cardinal depends on the autoprefixer, therefore you should use the Less Cardinal plugin with the Less `autoprefix` plugin. You can read more about the Less `autoprefix` plugin in the *Vendor-specific rules* section in *Chapter 1, Improving Web Development with Less*.

You can read more about the Less plugins in *Chapter 1, Improving Web Development with Less*. Note that the Less plugins described in the book only work in a `node.js` application (including Grunt and Gulp). However, sometimes they also work in a browser. When you compile the Less code in a different environment, you can't use these plugins and you should import the library code yourself.

Using Semantic UI with Less

Semantic can be used to build the frontends too. Just like Bootstrap, it contains the CSS components and modules. Components have been split into elements, collections, and views. Modules require not only CSS, but also JavaScript.

Semantic's name already implies that it pays attention to the semantics of HTML 5. It is also tag-agnostic, which means that you can use any HTML tags with the UI elements.

In the following code, you will find an HTML example that shows how Semantic is intended to be used:

```
<main class="ui three column grid">
  <aside class="column">1</aside>
  <section class="column">2</section>
  <section class="column">3</section>
</main>
```

You can easily install `npm` in the Semantic UI by running the following command:

```
> npm install semantic-ui
```

The Semantic UI uses Gulp to build a code. The Gulp build chain not only builds your code, but also offers you watch tasks. The Semantic UI uses Less and offers you over 3000 variables for customization. You can use themes to customize your builds. The Semantic UI offers two types of themes: packaged themes and site themes.

Each theme has got a `.variables` file and a `.overrides` file; both of these files are compiled by Less. Each component in Semantic inherits from the `site.variables` file. The theme's `.variables` file defines the custom values for the component's variables. Note that Less uses lazy loading and last declaration wins for variables, so you only have to redeclare the variables that are subject to modification. The Less code from the `.overrides` file compiles into the CSS code, which will be included after the default CSS code.

The packaged themes can be redistributed and used for more than one project, while the site themes can be used for the changes made to the UI elements of a single project.

After installing the Semantic UI as previously described, the `src` directory contains the files and directories like the ones shown as follows:

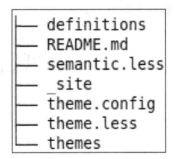

```
├── definitions
├── README.md
├── semantic.less
├── _site
├── theme.config
├── theme.less
└── themes
```

The folders and the files in the preceding formation can be used to customize the Semantic UI as described already. The `themes` directory contains many packaged themes. You can define the theme per component by using the code in the `theme.config` file.

The `theme.config` file contains, among other codes, the following code:

```
/* Elements */
@button       : 'default';
```

To use, for instance, the GitHub theme for your buttons, you should change the preceding code as shown here:

```
/* Elements */
@button       : 'github';
```

You can rebuild the code by running the following command:

```
> gulp build
```

After rebuilding the code, you will find that the `background-color` property for the `.ui.button` class in `build/semantic.css` has been changed from `#e0e0e0` to `#fafafa`. Using the GitHub theme will invoke many other changes in the compiled CSS code. You can use a site theme to override some variables of the GitHub theme. To override the `background-color` property, you should edit `src/site/elements/button.variables`. You can write the following Less code into this file:

```
/*******************************
    User Variable Overrides
*******************************/
@backgroundColor: orange;
```

After rebuilding the code, you will find that the `background-color` property for the `.ui.button` class has been changed to `orange`.

The Semantic UI not only compiles all of the codes into `build/semantic.css`, but also creates a CSS file for each component. After building the code, you can find these files in `dist/components`. The preceding step enables you to use a single component of the Semantic UI for the projects.

Deploying Ionic with Less

Ionic (`http://www.ionicframework.com`) and **Ratchet** (`http://goratchet.com`) are frameworks for building the hybrid mobile apps. The hybrid mobile apps are kinds of mobile web pages that are run as a native app. As these apps are web pages, you can use HTML5, JavaScript, and CSS to develop them. Both Ratchet and Ionic focus on the native or hybrid apps, instead of mobile websites. In this section, we will only discuss Ionic. Ionic apps are built by using HTML5.

The officially released version of Ionic comes with Sass now. In this section, you will learn how to develop the Ionic apps using Less.

For Ionic, a Less plugin is available at `https://github.com/bassjobsen/less-plugin-ionic`. You can install this plugin by running the following command on your console:

```
> npm install less-plugin-ionic
```

You should use this plugin with the Less `autoprefix` plugin.

Now you can compile a customized version of the Ionic's CSS code as follows:

```
> lessc file.less --ionic --autoprefix="Android >= 2.1,BlackBerry
>= 7,Chrome >= 20,Firefox >= 21,Explorer >= 10,iOS >= 3.2,Opera >
12,Safari > 6,OperaMobile >= 12.1,ChromeAndroid >= 40,FirefoxAndroid >=
30,ExplorerMobile >= 10"
```

Using Ionic's build chain with Less

When you start developing the mobile apps with Ionic and Less, you should keep the build chain intact and replace Sass with Less. In this section, we will shortly discuss the integration of Less with Ionic's build chain. You can read more about Less and Ionic at `https://github.com/bassjobsen/ionic-learn/blob/less/content/formulas/working-with-less/article.md`. The build process of Ionic uses Gulp. To compile the CSS code by using Less, you should add a new Less task to the `Gulpfile.js` file. The Gulp Less task should look like the code block shown here:

```
gulp.task('less', function(done) {

  var LessPluginIonic = require('less-plugin-ionic'),
  ioniclessc = new LessPluginIonic();

  var LessPluginAutoprefix = require('less-plugin-autoprefix'),
  autoprefix = new LessPluginAutoprefix({ browsers: ["Android >=
    2.1","BlackBerry >= 7","Chrome >= 20","Firefox >=
      21","Explorer >= 10","iOS >= 3.2","Opera > 12","Safari >
        6","OperaMobile >= 12.1","ChromeAndroid >=
          40","FirefoxAndroid >= 30","ExplorerMobile >= 10"] });

  gulp.src('./less/ionic.app.less')
  .pipe(less({
      plugins: [ioniclessc, autoprefix]
    }))
  .pipe(gulp.dest('./www/css/'))
  .pipe(minifyCss({
      keepSpecialComments: 0
  }))
  .pipe(rename({ extname: '.min.css' }))
  .pipe(gulp.dest('./www/css/'))
  .on('end', done);
})
```

The preceding Gulp task invokes the Less compiler that has the same plugins as described before. As the Less Ionic plugin imports all the required Less code for the framework, you only have to add your custom code to `less/ionic.app.less`. The `less/ionic.app.less` file can import any other Less file and make use of the mixins, variables, and classes, which have already been defined by the Ionic Less code provided with the Less Ionic plugin.

In the following screenshot, you will see an example of an Ionic app:

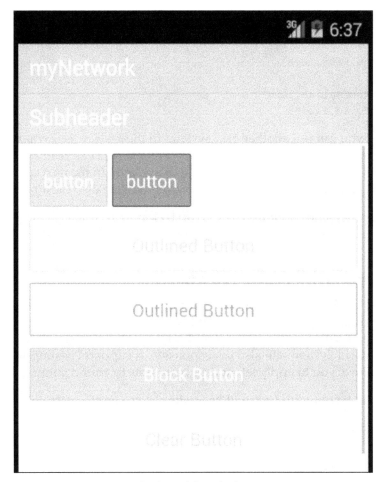

An example of a mobile UI built using Ionic

Frameworks for building your grids with Less

In the preceding section, you learned how to use the Bootstrap and Semantic UI to build complete frontends. In practice, for many projects, a grid alone will be enough to start. You have seen that Semantic's grid can be compiled in a single component easily. Bootstrap's grid can be compiled as a single component by using the following code snippet:

```
// Core variables and mixins
@import "variables.less";
@import "mixins.less";
// Reset
@import "normalize.less";
@import "grid.less";
```

Alternatively, you can use another grid system. In the *Making your grid responsive* section in *Chapter 5*, *Integrate Less in Your Own Projects*, you can read about the Zen grid, the Flexible box grid, and the `flexible.gs` system. In the next sections, the Semantic grid and the Skeleton framework system will be discussed briefly.

A list of the grid systems built using Less can be found at `http://lesscss.org/usage/#frameworks-using-less-grid-systems`.

The Semantic Grid System

The **Semantic Grid System** is very basic, but effective. After setting the `column` and `gutter` widths, choose the number of columns and switch between pixels and percentages; you will have a layout without any `.grid_x` classes on your markup. The Semantic Grid System will also be responsive. It supports nesting and push and pull, which allows you to apply left and right indents to your columns.

Defining a fluid layout with Less will be as simple as compiling the following code:

```
@import 'grid.less';
@columns: 12;
@column-width: 60;
@gutter-width: 20;

@total-width: 100%; // Switch from pixels to percentages
article {
  .column(9);
```

```
}
section {
  .column(3);
}
```

Further information about the Semantic Grid System can be found at `http://semantic.gs/`.

Skeleton's responsive boilerplate

In this book, you have already read about the large frameworks such as Bootstrap and Cardinal. Sometimes you don't need anything more than a grid for your project. Skeleton offers you a 12-column fluid grid with a maximum width of 960 px and a handful of the standard HTML elements.

You can download the Less code for Skeleton from `https://github.com/whatsnewsaes/Skeleton-Less`, or simply use the Less Skeleton plugin. You can install the Less Skeleton plugin by running the following command:

```
> npm install less-plugin-skeleton
```

Skeleton uses written numbers, such as one, two, and twelve, for the predefined grid classes. Some shorthand grid classes, such as one-third and one-half, are also available. You can use the following HTML snippet to get an impression of Skeleton's grid:

```html
<div class="container">
  <div class="row">
    <div class="one column">One</div>
    <div class="eleven columns">Eleven</div>
  </div>
  <div class="row">
    <div class="two columns">Two</div>
    <div class="ten columns">Ten</div>
  </div>
  <div class="row">
    <div class="one-third column">1/3</div>
    <div class="two-thirds column">2/3</div>
  </div>
  <div class="row">
    <div class="one-half column">1/2</div>
    <div class="one-half column">1/2</div>
  </div>
</div>
```

The preceding code can be inspected by loading `http://localhost/skeleton.html` in your browser. The `skeleton.html` file loads and compiles the Less code in `less/skeleton.less`. The `less/skeleton.less` file contains a Less code block as follows:

```
@import "Skeleton-Less/less/skeleton.less";

@container-width: 960px;

.column, .columns {
  border-radius: 15px;
  background-color: black;
  color: white;
  padding: 10px;
  border: 1px solid white;
}
```

The final result will look like the one shown here:

Example of Skeleton's grid

As you can see in the preceding screenshot, setting the maximum width of the grid is as easy as re-declaring the `@container-width` variable with a new value.

WordPress and Less

Nowadays, WordPress is not only used for weblogs, but it can also be used as a content management system for building a website.

The WordPress system, written in PHP, has been split into the core system, plugins, and themes. The plugins add additional functionalities to the system, and the themes handle the look and feel of a website built with WordPress. They work independently of each other and are also independent of the theme. The theme does not depend on plugins. WordPress themes define the global CSS for a website, but every plugin can also add its own CSS code.

The WordPress theme developers can use Less to compile the CSS code of the themes and the plugins.

Using the Sage theme by Roots with Less

Sage is a WordPress starter theme. You can use it to build your own theme. The theme is based on HTML5 Boilerplate (`http://html5boilerplate.com/`) and Bootstrap. Visit the Sage theme website at `https://roots.io/sage/`. Sage can also be completely built using Gulp.

 More information about how to use Gulp and Bower for the WordPress development can be found at `https://roots.io/sage/docs/theme-development/`.

After downloading Sage, the Less files can be found at `assets/styles/`. These files include Bootstrap's Less files, as described in *Chapter 6, Using the Bootstrap 3 Frontend Framework*. The `assets/styles/main.less` file imports the main Bootstrap Less file, `bootstrap.less`.

Now, you can edit `main.less` to customize your theme. You will have to rebuild the Sage theme after the changes you make. You can use all of the Bootstrap's variables to customize your build.

JBST with a built-in Less compiler

JBST is also a WordPress starter theme. JBST is intended to be used with the so-called child themes. More information about the WordPress child themes can be found at `https://codex.wordpress.org/Child_Themes`.

After installing JBST, you will find a Less compiler under **Appearance** in your **Dashboard** pane, as shown in the following screenshot:

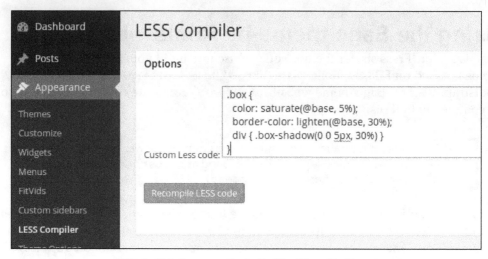

JBST's built-in Less compiler in the WordPress Dashboard

The built-in Less compiler can be used to fully customize your website using Less. Bootstrap also forms the skeleton of JBST, and the default settings are gathered by the a11y bootstrap theme mentioned earlier.

JBST's Less compiler can be used in the following different ways:

- First, the compiler accepts any custom-written Less (and CSS) code. For instance, to change the color of the h1 elements, you should simply edit and recompile the code as follows:

  ```
  h1 {color: red;}
  ```

- Secondly, you can edit Bootstrap's variables and (re)use Bootstrap's mixins. To set the background color of the navbar component and add a custom button, you can use the code block mentioned here in the Less compiler:

  ```
  @navbar-default-bg:           blue;
  .btn-colored {
    .button-variant(blue;red;green);
  }
  ```

- Thirdly, you can set JBST's built-in Less variables as follows:

  ```
  @footer_bg_color: black;
  ```

- Lastly, JBST has its own set of mixins. To set a custom font, you can edit the code as shown here:

```
.include-custom-font(@family: arial,@font-path, @path:
    @custom-font-dir, @weight: normal, @style: normal);
```

In the preceding code, the parameters mentioned were used to set the font name (`@family`) and the path name to the font files (`@path`/`@font-path`). The `@weight` and `@style` parameters set the font's properties. For more information, visit `https://github.com/bassjobsen/Boilerplate-JBST-Child-Theme`.

More Less code blocks can also be added to a special file (`wpless2css/wpless2css.less` or `less/custom.less`); these files will give you the option to add, for example, a library of prebuilt mixins, such as the one discussed in *Chapter 4, Testing Your Code and Using Prebuilt Mixins Libraries*. After adding the library using this file, the mixins can also be used with the built-in compiler.

The Semantic UI WordPress theme

The Semantic UI, as discussed earlier, offers its own WordPress plugin. The plugin can be downloaded from `https://github.com/ProjectCleverWeb/Semantic-UI-WordPress`. After installing and activating this theme, you can use your website directly with the Semantic UI. With the default setting, your website will look like the following screenshot:

Website built with the Semantic UI WordPress theme

WordPress plugins and Less

As discussed earlier, the WordPress plugins have their own CSS. This CSS will be added to the page like a normal style sheet, as shown here:

```
<link rel='stylesheet' id='plugin-name'
  href='//domain/wp-content/plugin-name/plugin-name.css?ver=2.1.2'
    type='text/css' media='all' />
```

Unless a plugin provides the Less files for their CSS code, it will not be easy to manage its styles with Less.

The WP Less to CSS plugin

The **WP Less to CSS** plugin, which can be found at `http://wordpress.org/plugins/wp-less-to-css/`, offers the possibility of styling your WordPress website with Less. As seen earlier, you can enter the Less code along with the built-in compiler of JBST. This code will then be compiled into the website's CSS. This plugin compiles Less with the PHP Less compiler, `Less.php`.

Using Less with the Play framework

The Play framework helps you in building lightweight and scalable web applications by using Java or Scala. It will be interesting to learn how to integrate Less with the workflow of the Play framework. The differences between Java and Scala are beyond the scope of this book, but you can read more about this at `http://www.toptal.com/scala/why-should-i-learn-scala`. Also, the discussion of the installation process of the Play framework has not been handled in detail in this book. You can install the Play framework from `https://www.playframework.com/`. To learn more about the Play framework, you can also read, *Learning Play! Framework 2, Andy Petrella, Packt Publishing*.

 To read Petrella's book, visit `https://www.packtpub.com/web-development/learning-play-framework-2`.

To run the Play framework, you need JDK 6 or later. The easiest way to install the Play framework is by using the **Typesafe activator** tool. After installing the activator tool, you can run the following command:

```
> activator new my-first-app play-scala
```

The preceding command will install a new app in the my-first-app directory. Using the play-java option instead of the play-scala option in the preceding command will lead to the installation of a Java-based app. Later on, you can add the Scala code in a Java app or the Java code in a Scala app.

After installing a new app with the activator command, you can run it by using the following commands:

```
cd my-first-app

activator run
```

Now, you can find your app at http://localhost:9000.

To enable the Less compilation, you should simply add the sbt-less plugin to your plugins.sbt file as follows:

```
addSbtPlugin("com.typesafe.sbt" % "sbt-less" % "1.0.6")
```

After enabling the plugin, you can edit the build.sbt file so as to configure Less. You should save the Less files into app/assets/stylesheets/. Note that each file in app/assets/stylesheets/ will compile into a separate CSS file.

The CSS files will be saved in public/stylesheets/ and should be called in your templates with the HTML code shown here:

```
<link rel="stylesheet"
  href="@routes.Assets.at("stylesheets/main.css")">
```

In case you are using a library with more files imported into the main file, you can define the filters in the build.sbt file. The filters for these so-called partial source files can look like the following code:

```
includeFilter in (Assets, LessKeys.less) := "*.less"
excludeFilter in (Assets, LessKeys.less) := "_*.less"
```

The preceding filters ensure that the files starting with an underscore are not compiled into CSS.

Using Bootstrap with the Play framework

Bootstrap is a CSS framework. You can read more about Bootstrap in *Chapter 6, Using the Bootstrap 3 Frontend Framework*. Bootstrap's Less code includes many files. Keeping your code up-to-date by using partials, as described in the preceding section, will not work well. Alternatively, you can use **WebJars** with Play for this purpose. To enable the Bootstrap WebJar, you should add the code shown here to your `build.sbt` file:

```
libraryDependencies += "org.webjars" % "bootstrap" % "3.3.2"
```

When using the Bootstrap WebJar, you can import Bootstrap into your project as follows:

```
@import "lib/bootstrap/less/bootstrap.less";
```

AngularJS and Less

AngularJS is a structural framework for dynamic web apps. It extends the HTML syntax, and this enables you to create dynamic web views. Of course, you can use AngularJS with Less. You can read more about AngularJS at `https://angularjs.org/`.

The HTML code shown here will give you an example of what repeating the HTML elements with AngularJS will look like:

```
<!doctype html>
<html ng-app>
  <head>
    <title>My Angular App</title>
  </head>
  <body ng-app>

    <ul>
      <li ng-repeat="item in [1,2,3]">{{ item }}</li>
    </ul>
    <script
      src="https://ajax.googleapis.com/ajax/libs/angularjs/1.3.12/
        angular.min.js"></script>
  </body>
</html>
```

The preceding HTML code can also be found in the `angular.html` file from the downloads section of this chapter. This code should make your page look like the following screenshot:

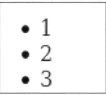

Repeating the HTML elements with AngularJS

The ngBoilerplate system

The **ngBoilerplate** system is an easy way to start a project with AngularJS. The project comes with a directory structure for your application and a Grunt build process, including a Less task and other useful libraries.

To start your project, you should simply run the following commands on your console:

```
> git clone git://github.com/ngbp/ngbp
> cd ngbp
> sudo npm -g install grunt-cli karma bower
> npm install
> bower install
> grunt watch
```

And then, open `///path/to/ngbp/build/index.html` in your browser.

After installing ngBoilerplate, you can write the Less code into `src/less/main.less`. By default, only `src/less/main.less` will be compiled into CSS; other libraries and other codes should be imported into this file.

Meteor and Less

Meteor is a complete open-source platform for building web and mobile apps in pure JavaScript. Meteor focuses on fast development. You can publish your apps for free on Meteor's servers.

Meteor is available for Linux and OS X. You can also install it on Windows.

Installing Meteor is as simple as running the following command on your console:

```
> curl https://install.meteor.com | /bin/sh
```

You should install the Less package for compiling the CSS code of the app with Less. You can install the Less package by running the command shown here:

```
> meteor add less
```

Note that the Less package compiles every file with the `.less` extension into CSS. For each file with the `.less` extension, a separate CSS file is created. When you use the partial Less files that should only be imported (with the `@import` directive) and not compiled into the CSS code itself, you should give these partials the `.import.less` extension.

When using the CSS frameworks or libraries with many partials, renaming the files by adding the `.import.less` extension will hinder you in updating your code. Also running postprocess tasks for the CSS code is not always possible.

Many packages for Meteor are available at `https://atmospherejs.com/`. Some of these packages can help you solve the issue with using partials mentioned earlier. To use Bootstrap, as described in *Chapter 5*, *Integrating Less in Your Own Projects*, you can use the `meteor-bootstrap` package. The `meteor-bootstrap` package can be found at `https://github.com/Nemo64/meteor-bootstrap`. The `meteor-bootstrap` package requires the installation of the Less package. Other packages provide you postprocsess tasks, such as autoprefixing your code.

Ruby on rails and Less

Ruby on Rails, or **Rails**, for short is a web application development framework written in the Ruby language. Although installing Rails is not that difficult, it is beyond the scope of this book.

Those who want to start developing with Ruby on Rails can read the *Getting Started with Rails* guide, which can be found at `http://guides.rubyonrails.org/getting_started.html`.

In this section, you can read how to integrate Less into a Ruby on Rails app.

After installing the tools and components required for starting with Rails, you can launch a new application by running the following command on your console:

```
> rails new blog
```

Now, you should integrate Less with Rails. You can use `less-rails` (https://github.com/metaskills/less-rails) to bring Less to Rails. Open the `Gemfile` file, comment on the `sass-rails` gem, and add the `less-rails` gem, as shown here:

```
#gem 'sass-rails', '~> 5.0'
gem 'less-rails' # Less
gem 'therubyracer' # Ruby
```

Then, create a controller called `welcome` with an action called `index` by running the following command:

```
> bin/rails generate controller welcome index
```

The preceding command will generate `app/views/welcome/index.html.erb`. Open `app/views/welcome/index.html.erb` and make sure that it contains the HTML code as shown here:

```
<h1>Welcome#index</h1>
<p>Find me in app/views/welcome/index.html.erb</p>
```

The next step is to create a file, `app/assets/stylesheets/welcome.css.less`, with the Less code. The Less code in `app/assets/stylesheets/welcome.css.less` looks as follows:

```
@color: red;
h1 {
  color: @color;
}
```

Now, start a web server with the following command:

```
> bin/rails server
```

Finally, you can visit the application at `http://localhost:3000/`. The application should look like the example shown here:

The Rails app

Alternative compilers for compiling your Less code

With the growing popularity of Less, the Less compiler has also been ported to other languages. These ports can be used to compile Less with native language calls. Keep in mind that these ports will usually lag behind the official JavaScript implementation, so you may find that they don't have the recent Less features. You may also realize that these compilers are not able to compile the native JavaScript expressions within backticks, as mentioned in *Chapter 3, Nested Rules, Operations, and Built-in Functions*.

The Less.php compiler

This PHP port of the official Less processor can be downloaded from http://lessphp.gpeasy.com/. You have already seen an example of its usage: the WP Less to the CSS plugin has been built with it. Less.php also implements caching for faster compilation.

Although Less.php offers the possibility of creating CSS dynamically, you should still precompile the CSS for production in most cases. WordPress is also written in PHP, so in the case of the WordPress plugin, Less can be compiled without using system calls.

In the following code, you will find an example that will show you how to compile, customize, and use Bootstrap on a website written in PHP:

```php
<?php
require 'less.php/Cache.php';
Less_Cache::$cache_dir = '/var/www/mysite/writable_folder';
$files = array();
$files['/var/www/mysite/bootstrap/bootstrap.less'] =
  '/mysite/bootstrap/';
$files['/var/www/mysite/custom/my.less'] = '/mysite/custom/';
$css_file_name = Less_Cache::Get( $files );
echo '<link rel="stylesheet" type="text/css"
  href="/mysite/writable_folder/'.$css_file_name.'">';
```

An alternative PHP Less compiler, lessphp, is available at http://leafo.net/lessphp/.

The .less compiler for .NET apps

The `.less` compiler is a complete port for the JavaScript Less library for the .NET platform. If you want to statically compile your files, you can use the `dotless.Compiler.exe` compiler, which is included with it. You can read more about .NET at `http://www.dotlesscss.org/`.

You can use files with the `.less` extension on your web page by adding a new HTTP handler to the `Web.Config` file as follows:

```
<add type="dotless.Core.LessCssHttpHandler,dotless.Core"
  validate="false" path="*.Less" verb="*" />
```

The `.less` compiler can easily be installed with NuGet. Open the Visual Studio Package Manager Console and run command shown here:

```
> Install-Package dotless
```

Cassette offers you an alternative manner in which you can install Less .NET. Cassette automatically sorts, concatenates, minifies, caches, and compiles your assets for the .WEB apps. You can install Less along with Cassette and NuGet by running the following command:

```
> Install-Package Cassette.Less
```

Web developers can also use Web Essentials. Web Essentials adds useful features to Visual Studio. The Less extension compiles the Less code into a custom folder and enables you to generate a preview. Web Essentials uses the `node` Less compiler, and it always uses the latest version. You can read more about Web Essentials and Less at `http://vswebessentials.com/features/less`.

 On the Less website (`http://lesscss.org/usage/`), you will find many other libraries, tools, and frameworks for developing Less.

Summary

In this chapter, you learned how to use Less with Cardinal, Semantic UI, and Ionic. You were also introduced to the other grids and the frameworks built using Less. You have seen how to use Less with WordPress, Play, Meteor, AngularJS, Ruby on Rails, and you saw how to use the alternative compilers for your project.

This is the last chapter of this book. In this book, you learned how to use Less for your projects. You saw how variables, mixins, and built-in functions can help you in reusing your code. With Less, you can nest the style rules that make your code more intuitive and readable. After reading this book, you know that you don't have to write all the code yourself, when you can use the prebuilt mixins written by others. Finally, you obtained the information on how to start projects from scratch with Less. You also learned about integrating Less with WordPress, Bootstrap, and other tools. Now, you are really ready to start developing Less. Congratulations! You have enabled yourself to work better and faster by using Less for your projects and will save more time when designing tasks.

Index

Block, Element, Modifier (BEM)
  reference link 40
  syntax, assumptions 41
Bootflat project
  reference link 72
Bootstrap
  about 187
  default theme 188
  project, building with Grunt 194-196
  references 188, 211
  theming, with Less 210
  URL, for source code 119
  using, with Play framework 228
Bootstrap 3 187
Bootstrap grid
  about 189-191
  mixins 191-193
  variables 191-193
Bootstrap Less plugin 198
Bootswatch
  about 199
  URL 199
border-radius property
  used, for building rounded corners 18-21
Bower, for WordPress development
  reference link 223
bower resolve plugin
  reference link 14
box-shadow mixin 58, 115, 116
box-sizing mixin 57
box-sizing property 29-33
browser compatibility
  reference link 7
built-in functions
  about 102
  color functions 105, 106
  colors, manipulating 108
  darken() 107
  JavaScript functions 102, 103
  Less, extending with custom functions 114
  lighten() 107
  list functions 103-105
  type, evaluating of input value 113

C

CamelCase 48
Can I use
  URL 17
Cardinal
  URL, for downloading 214
Cardinal CSS 214
cascade, CSS
  about 3
  global rules 3, 4
center-content mixins 58
child themes, WordPress
  reference link 223
Chrome's developer tools 120-122
classes
  about 90, 91, 205-209
  using 87-89
clean-css plugin
  reference link 14
clean-css postprocessor
  reference link 36
clearfix mixin
  about 58
  using 166
Clearless library
  URL 127
  using 134-137
CodeKIT 39
color blending, Less
  about 111
  reference link 112
color
  functions, using 106
  operating on 99, 100
  operations 108
  reference link 110
  reference link, for keyword names 106
color schemes, with 1pxdeep 211
color theory
  reference link 108
comma-separated value (CSV) 20, 61, 101

navigation structure 81
nested comments 44
nested grids
  building 168, 169
nested rules
  working with 82-86
ngBoilerplate system 229
Node.js
  reference link 34
normalize.css file
  reference link 22
npm
  reference link 34
npm import plugin
  reference link 14
numbers
  operating on 99, 100

O

object-oriented CSS
  reference links 195

P

parametric mixins
  about 58
  default values 59, 60
parent selector
  referencing, with & symbol 92-97
Play framework
  Bootstrap, using with 228
  Less, using with 226, 227
  reference link 226
Pleeease
  about 37
  URL 37
PostCSS autoprefixer
  about 17
  reference link 17
post-process plugins
  autoprefix 14
  clean-css 14

Preboot library
  URL 127
  using 137, 138
Preboot's grid system
  mixins 175
  using 174-178
prebuilt mixins libraries
  3L library, using 133
  about 127, 128
  Clearless library, using 134-137
  gradients creating, Less Elements
      used 128-131
  layouts creating, Less Elements
      used 128-131
  Less-bidi library 141, 142
  Less Hat library 131, 132
  lesshat mixin, for less.js plugin 133
  more-or-less library, using 139-141
  Preboots prebuilt mixins, using 137, 138
  URL 127
Prefixfree library
  URL 198
pre-process plugins
  Bootstrap 14
project migration, Less
  CSS code, converting 156, 157
  files, organizing 155
property merging 101

R

Ratchet
  URL 217
Respond.js
  about 162
  URL 162
Responsinator
  URL 161
responsive design
  about 157
  fluid layout, creating 158, 159

Thank you for buying
Less Web Development Essentials
Second Edition

About Packt Publishing

Packt, pronounced 'packed', published its first book, *Mastering phpMyAdmin for Effective MySQL Management*, in April 2004, and subsequently continued to specialize in publishing highly focused books on specific technologies and solutions.

Our books and publications share the experiences of your fellow IT professionals in adapting and customizing today's systems, applications, and frameworks. Our solution-based books give you the knowledge and power to customize the software and technologies you're using to get the job done. Packt books are more specific and less general than the IT books you have seen in the past. Our unique business model allows us to bring you more focused information, giving you more of what you need to know, and less of what you don't.

Packt is a modern yet unique publishing company that focuses on producing quality, cutting-edge books for communities of developers, administrators, and newbies alike. For more information, please visit our website at www.packtpub.com.

About Packt Open Source

In 2010, Packt launched two new brands, Packt Open Source and Packt Enterprise, in order to continue its focus on specialization. This book is part of the Packt Open Source brand, home to books published on software built around open source licenses, and offering information to anybody from advanced developers to budding web designers. The Open Source brand also runs Packt's Open Source Royalty Scheme, by which Packt gives a royalty to each open source project about whose software a book is sold.

Writing for Packt

We welcome all inquiries from people who are interested in authoring. Book proposals should be sent to author@packtpub.com. If your book idea is still at an early stage and you would like to discuss it first before writing a formal book proposal, then please contact us; one of our commissioning editors will get in touch with you.

We're not just looking for published authors; if you have strong technical skills but no writing experience, our experienced editors can help you develop a writing career, or simply get some additional reward for your expertise.

[PACKT] open source ✤
community experience distilled
PUBLISHING

Learning Less.js

ISBN: 978-1-78216-066-3   Paperback: 342 pages

Develop attractive CSS styles efficiently, using the Less CSS preprocessor

1. Use the robust features of the LESS library to write CSS styles in an organized manner.

2. Simplify your development workflow by using LESS when working with frameworks or content management systems.

3. Harness the power of LESS to build websites, using practical examples.

Instant LESS CSS Preprocessor How-to

ISBN: 978-1-78216-376-3   Paperback: 80 pages

Practical, hands-on recipes to write more efficient CSS, with the help of the LESS CSS Preprocessor library

1. Learn something new in an Instant! A short, fast, focused guide delivering immediate results.

2. Use mixins, functions, and variables to dynamically auto-generate styles, based on minimal existing values.

3. Use the power of LESS to produce style sheets dynamically, or incorporate precompiled versions into your code.

Please check **www.PacktPub.com** for information on our titles

Rapid LESS
Reme Le Hane

[PACKT]
VIDEO

Rapid LESS [Video]

ISBN: 978-1-78398-976-8   Duration: 01:12 hours

Write less code, time-saving cheats, and design a professional website using the LESS CSS preprocessor

1. Design a top-notch website with one of the best CSS pre-processors.

2. Take your CSS skills a step higher by using LESS and write lesser code.

3. Learn about variables, mixins, nesting, operations and functions to design your website in quick easy steps.

Less Web Development Essentials

Use CSS preprocessing to streamline the development and maintenance of your web applications

Foreword by Alexis Seller, creator of Less

Bass Jobsen   PACKT open source

Less Web Development Essentials

ISBN: 978-1-78398-146-5   Paperback: 202 pages

Use CSS preprocessing to streamline the development and maintenance of your web applications

1. Produce clear, concise, and well-constructed code that compiles into standard compliant CSS.

2. Explore the core attributes of Less and learn how to integrate them into your site.

3. Optimize Twitter's Bootstrap to efficiently develop web apps and sites.

Please check **www.PacktPub.com** for information on our titles